# TABLE OI

The trademarks that are used are without any consent, and the publication of the trademark is without permission or backing by the trademark owner. All trademarks and brands within this book are for clarifying purposes only and are owned by the owners themselves, not affiliated with this document.

# INTRODUCTION

Marketers argue that brands have long captured markets and the minds of users. However, not every trademark is a brand, and not all companies strive to create their brand.

Is brand Identity that important?

Suppose a company occupies its niche in the regional market, belongs to small or medium-sized businesses, does not seek to develop and master new sales markets. In that case, it can successfully realize itself in a specific niche until those who have already understood how important and profitable it is to create their brand begin to replace it.

The answer to why branding is so important is that most consumers opt for brands with strong associations. Consumers are guaranteed to give preference to goods and services from a well-known manufacturer in a competitive environment.

The company's personal brand significantly increases its value; some brands cost more than the budget of small countries. The profits of the 5 largest corporations are twice the combined GDP of the poorest countries. Hence, it is clear that brands have a great impact on the global economy and consumer consciousness.

What branding gives

At its core, branding is a way to manipulate the minds of consumers. It gives them the impression of the exceptional value of the products, which allows them to sell them at a higher price than competitors' products. According to research, a personal brand allows a company to receive about 80% of the margin people are always willing to pay for the brand.

You also need to understand why branding is important to keep customers connected to products and services, despite better offers from competitors. The emotional attachment of buyers to products, which is created through strong associations, is a way of maintaining customer loyalty despite competitors' intrigues.

By studying branding: why companies create brands, researchers have found lower advertising costs. Launching new goods and services to the marketplace or entering new sales markets becomes an easier task for a well-known company than for companies without a name. The presence of a personal brand in a company increases staff motivation; employees are more willing to work in well-known companies.

Branding is primarily of interest to companies with plans for a long-term stay in the market, taking leadership positions there, and having a certain development strategy and healthy ambitions. A lot is described as the prospects for branding identity in this blueprint with development, effective business models, and branding tools. If you have any inquiries regarding the need or creation of a Brand Identity, you need to do your best to complete this blueprint to develop a strategy for your brand and identify the perfect approach to craft and design an Irresistible Story Brand Business promotion without any hassle.

Sit, relax, and enjoy the reading …

# CHAPTER 1

## Brand Identity

### *1.1 Definition of Brand*

A brand can be defined as a trademark with which a product was marked. Usually, most marketers understand a brand as a name, term, sign, symbol, color, image, sound, or rather a combination thereof, designed to differentiate a product (service) from competitors' products.

During the first few years, about 80 - 90% of products that first appeared on the market disappear from the market for various reasons. One of them, for example, is that the buyer did not understand why they were needed. There are only products that have the marketing characteristics, values and promises required by the market, in the promotion of which the brand owner has put some, often quite significant efforts.

Often the concept of a brand is understood as different:

a). The brand is a prestigious, popular, well-known trademark. A brand is perceived as energy (Brand energy) a measure of the ability of a brand to influence a customer, associated with its customer loyalty. Brand as a promise (Brand promise) the benefits and benefits that consumers expect to receive from a given brand. Brand values is a term used to describe the financial value of a brand. Brand as emotional capital (Brand-related emotional capital) is a reflection of the emotional loyalty of employees to the company's brand.

b). A brand is a source of added value, in addition to that which is provided by the product as such (when only its consumer properties are meant). This also includes the concept of "product-plus", which considers a brand (trademark) as a kind of "added value" to a product (service). Brand as equity (Brand equity) a concept that considers a brand as a tangible and intangible asset that can be bought and sold. If a brand is rich and robust, it means that it has a lot of capital.

c). Brand as a symbol of a trademark, the sum of all the mental connections that are formed between buyers and brand owners. A brand is an attempt at individualization (Brand personality, brand individuality) the personification of the brand image in the mind of the consumer, expressed in terms of individual traits of a person.

## *1.2 What is Brand Identity?*

Brand identity: the unity of style elements that identify the belonging of everything on which these elements are placed (goods, means of communication, communication messages) to a particular company and distinguish it from competitors.

The brand identity is the basis of the company's communication policy, since it provides a visual and semantic unity of goods and services, all information coming from the company. Moreover, the brand identity ensures the unity of all products of the company; on the other hand, the brand identity opposes the company and its products to competitors and their products.

The brand identity is one of the tools for forming a brand and at the same time, an element of branding. The concept of brand identity is closely related to the concept of image. The brand identity is a means of forming the company's image, which distinguishes the company and confirms the reliability of the company.

The main task of the brand identity is to make the company's products recognizable and different from the products of other companies, to increase competitive advantages, propagandize and advertising effect, and to protect goods from counterfeiting.

The brand identity can include a whole complex of different elements of influence on the target audience: visual, psychological, sound, and sometimes some others. Brand identity elements mean a combination of a trademark, logo, color, font and their use in the design of business papers and communications.

## 1.3 What Is the Big Deal About Brand Identities?

Identity is considered an essential attribute of a marketing company; it helps to stand out among hundreds of similar offers. The harmonious combination of shades and basic design attracts attention, permanently imprinted in the memory of potential customers. The issue of personal identification was and remained a priority. Therefore, the use of this marketing tool is becoming increasingly relevant, because the modern market is overflowing with the same offers, in the mass of which yours can be lost.

Companies spend a lot of money on brand identity. A lot of professional designers, marketers and advertisers are engaged in the development of brand identity. Everyone is talking about him. Why and who needs it? Is it worth the money invested in it? And how long can a good brand identity last?

To answer some of these questions, you need to refer to the definition of brand identity. Brand identity is nothing more than a distinctive feature, identification. Thus, a brand identity is not just something beautiful that can be placed in a company's advertisement. It is primarily a graphical expression of how the company differs from other companies.

The brand identity not only creates the image of the company but also forms a certain ideal to which the company aspires. It turns out that the brand identity is needed both by the company and its customers. Companies to stand out from the competition. Clients so that they can quickly identify the company, its product or services, among other offers.

Naturally, the development of a brand identity is quite expensive. As you already understood from the definition, creating a brand identity is not just about drawing a picture to make it beautiful. An arbitrarily created brand identity that has nothing to do with the company's activities, its characteristics, can even harm the company and its products.

Therefore, it is quite logical that you will have to pay a lot of money for a good, high-quality, well-thought-out brand identity. But don't worry, they will come back to you as buyers of your products. Of course, you can save money and order an inexpensive brand identity. In this case, you risk paying twice, and the total amount will be much higher than if you immediately made a good identity. Why? It's very simple to explain.

So, you have released a product or service to the market under a particular brand identity. Then your company began to develop, and you realized that the current brand identity did not suit it at all. Only one way out to develop a new brand identity and this is again costs, and not only for development but also for the formation in the minds of customers of a new image of your company, that is, for advertising.

A good brand identity can last not years, decades. Think of the big corporations for example, Pepsi, Coca-Cola, Mercedes, Samsung and others. Their brand identity has remained unchanged over the years. Of course, there have been minor changes, but in general, they use all the same colors as many years ago.

## *1.4 The Public and Your Brand Identity*

The development of trademarks and of branding itself has gone quite a challenging, but as it seems now a logical path. This path is akin to the development of society itself, its unification, globalization in all its positive and negative aspects. There are political, economic, informational and social components here. It is the last component, which speaks of structural and communication changes in society, that interests me most. It is also necessary to note the change, the evolution of consciousness concerning the very material consumption of those people whom we now call consumers. Let's make a reservation right away that by consumers, we mean those who are in one way or another connected with the capacious concept and philosophy of modern consumption.

The evolution of an idea, a brand image, and then a brand can be rather conditionally divided into three stages: pre-industrial, industrial and informational. The division between these stages is relative, and there are no clear time boundaries between them, but an approximate time frame can be indicated.

The industrial stage of development, from which, in fact, the formation of brands in their modern understanding began, began to gradually replace the pre-industrial, prehistoric stage of brands, from the middle of the 19th century to the beginning of the 20th century. The last, informational stage, is at its beginning now in the well-developed (capitalist) countries of the world.

## *Pre-Industrial Stage*

The first stage of the still potential life of brands in ordinary goods is indicated by the following features of the pre-industrial, agrarian society: regional autonomy, fragmentation of small administrative entities, cultural monopoly of the ruling class and the capital, the

11

insignificance of the masses for culture and politics, imperious vertical integration and membership in the society, following kinship, caste, religion.

Initially, in the regular market for ordinary buyers, there were simple salted salt, simple wheat, tow, soap and several hundred other products named, as well as the product itself. But these products have not yet been identified and connected with the buyer psychologically and emotionally, their individual and personal character have not been created, their non-product essence has not been expressed.

In general, everything that makes up the essence of the brand and helps to be born and come true consumer dreams did not yet exist. The point was just that all these everyday products were sold for the most "mundane" consumption, to satisfy physiological needs and did not have any particular independent values.

They were just a bar of soap, i.e. the fact that it washed well and did not have such unique additional attributes as the ability to charm or turn everything into beauty. At the same time, for example, each loaf of bread had its smell, taste, weight, etc. depending on who baked it. In this sense, all products were unique, in contrast to the products of industrial society, with their mass and standard nature. Products in pre-industrial society performed exclusively utilitarian functions.

However, the consumer was not yet a consumer in the modern sense: he was not exposed to advertising influence, did not absorb brand ideas through marketing communications and advertising. A person, for the most part, bought a product only to satisfy his needs for food, drink, safety, etc., that is, guided by practical considerations, which were realized through impersonal goods.

Thus, the goods of the pre-industrial period served only the urgent material needs of people, as opposed to other non-commercial values that satisfied higher needs (psychological, social, cultural, spiritual): a person's relationship with family, friends, state, religion and others.

## *Industrial Stage*

At the second, industrial stage, with the formation of industry, its growth and the disappearance of handicraft and handicraft production, goods become more and more standard, unified and technological. In general, regional autonomy is decreasing; society is becoming more integrated, thanks to the development of economic and industrial ties, uniform legislation and general government at the state level.

The ruling class's monopoly on culture is becoming a thing of the past, the level of education of the population rises (mass education appears), and access to cultural values is formally open to everyone. Membership in a society is already primarily determined by a person's language and abilities. The economy is horizontally integrated, and its role in social development becomes leading along with some ideas, which quickly spread to the whole world through the media that have become powerful means. Production gradually becomes mass and cheaper; hence mass consumption arises and begins to take shape.

The leading role of the economy leads to the fact that consumer behavior begins to be promoted in every possible way as something the best in life. Gradually, under the influence of the ideas broadcast through the promoted brands, people develop a new idea of wealth, happiness, development and most importantly, life itself and all that it consists of. This change occurs sequentially: from the lowest values of people, such as physiological needs, safety, to higher ones, such as self-esteem and self-realization.

In new, emerging representations, the brand becomes an integral element and participant, but at first only as a brand of one product.

Products that become similar in price and quality have no choice but to gradually replace their physical attributes with emotional ones when serving them to the consumer—social, aesthetic. At the same time, the brand uses not only material but also psychological, emotional, social needs of people, i.e. the possession of a branded product becomes an integral part of not so much satisfied physical as social and psychological comfort.

Everything that happens to people under the influence of brands ultimately leads to a single strategic marketing goal to increase profits with the growth of brand capital and differs from brand to brand only in tactical moments. Simultaneously, some of the most successful brands begin to grow and expand, capturing more and more new products and forming whole lines of different, but still quite similar products. It is natural that over time, the brand's connection with its consumer is strengthened, provided that the brand's diverse marketing communications are consistent and developed.

Throughout the past, twentieth century, generation after generation, people grew up whose personal and social norms, and values are increasingly becoming consumer on the one hand and controlled through marketing communications on the other, people, thinking in terms and within brands. Under the influence of ideas of strong brands and ideas of an industrial consumer society, there is a change in the expression of moral and moral norms of a human consumer. There is a substitution of what is used to express the irrational and existential values that are present a priori in the minds of people.

Now they are beginning to be more realized through the consumer culture and the "special" values of the product (brand). In the industrial stage, the gap between the role of man, which he plays in society, and his essence begins to disappear, he becomes, including for himself, what he consumes through which the irrational and existential values that are present a priori in the minds of people are expressed.

## *Information Stage*

The saturation of the established consumer society with goods, the development of the scientific and technological revolution, means of communication and other factors lead to the formation of an information society, characterized by the importance of information and a network like a horizontal organization. Important characteristic features of the information society are: the priority of the tertiary sector of the economy (services, science), an increase in the rhythm and speed of life; information technology makes it possible to eliminate large-scale production.

The main resource of the information society is becoming knowledge and science with their point impact, in contrast to the industrial one, where they were production power and high energies. The main element of the information society is not interaction with nature as in a pre-industrial society and not its transformation as in an industrial society, but interaction,

At the informational stage of the development of society and brands, many goods appear that are in one way or another different from each other, at least at first glance. They are produced in different small batches, often under the same brand name. At the same time, brands are expanding, capturing for themselves, uniting fundamentally different products with their ideas. The very way of life of a person changes, the main thing is that a person ceases to have constancy for the whole life, and his life can change extremely quickly. Neither profession, nor education, nor work, nor even something personal is now final for a person.

15

And in this, he is greatly helped by brands: supporting people, allowing them to change their style when they change quickly, and therefore the perception of a person by society and oneself. The main conflict of society from the sphere of production (as it was in industrial society) is shifted to the sphere of consumption, i.e. the struggle is no longer for the means of production, but for working conditions, wages. Moving away from the mass character of the industrial society, saturation of consumers in the physical and social terms, bring to life brands that include values that are increasingly close to the top of Maslow's pyramid, which does not prevent these brands, including containing and declaring lower values in the pyramid.

These brands offer the consumer a whole complex and coherent set of values and even beliefs. As a result of presenting oneself to the consumer in a complex manner, at a more significant number of pyramid levels, and, accordingly, increasing loyalty, trademarks begin to unite more and more products and product categories.

They start talking, and the consumer sees in them an opportunity for self-respect, self-expression and, as a result, self-realization. They help the consumer to absorb from them such beliefs as belief in goodness and justice, or, conversely, selfishness and arrogance. Consumers begin to pursue their high moral, emotional and aesthetic needs through brand awareness after meeting them on a physical and social level. All brand communications, including advertising, become less informative of the consumer about any properties and attributes of the product, as much as they evoke emotions and attach them to the lifestyle that the well-built brand itself is most consistent with (the image component in advertising is growing).

Considering the increase in the amount of information and the constant increase in the informational, managerial and psychological stress load on a person, the brand begins to offer a person a solution to a set of problems: physical, emotional, social, cultural and even spiritual plans, thus taking its consumer under protection, offering under his name is a lot of different goods. By choosing this or that brand with its multilevel advantages for "solving all problems" and showing further loyalty to it, the consumer gets rid, firstly, of the known risk when buying an unknown brand (which can lead to unpredictable results), and secondly, protects itself and is eliminated from a massive flow of information for making a purchase decision and in general about lifestyle.

## Dry Residue

The psychological mechanism of consumer loyalty to the brand lies in familiarization and partly in identification with the brand itself and its ideas. Commitment arises when a person is impressed by what he thinks, "thinks" about him and "does" the brand for him. A person consumes the product that appears to him as a brand that contains not so much good physical attributes of the product (despite the fact that all products have approximately the same quality and characteristics) as some "higher" properties that offer a solution to the possible development of a given person.

A person for himself and those around him become a bearer of the brand's values and faith, "communes" with him as in a religious ceremony, becomes a part of communication and further brand promotion. Thus, for a while, the consumer has a feeling of approaching or even achieving the goal of his existence, of joining the higher, which is then replaced by a new "hunger" of consumption, stimulated by marketing communications, and most importantly, by the very philosophy of consumption.

Thus, brands, on the one hand, gradually became instruments of a person's search for a higher, and sometimes replaced the existential search itself, putting themselves in the place of higher values, taking

17

a place that previously belonged, for example, to religion. Strong brands act similarly to the good old religion, though simplifying the path a little and leading a person along with it at first glance with greater ease. At the same time, they require the same as religion energy, worship, faith.

The goal of marketing communications, therefore, is a developed fetishism in the form of substitution and substitution of a person's emotional, social, spiritual search for easily attainable relevant aspects of the brand in exchange for his money. This must be extended to as many people as possible. For this, the brand must be present and attractive at more levels of the pyramid from the brand-product to the brand-religion and lead a person, to seek his acceptance from him at the highest possible level and more of the quantity (which will provide the brand with greater loyalty).

The brand and the person-consumer seem to have changed places in comparison with the person and the product. That is, instead of serving a product to a person, a brand takes the place of a person, demanding from him "service" to himself, attention and time, giving him a sense of peace in return from the illusion of achieving a goal, which a person from the "good-brand" world has now transferred to the brand through marketing.

But for this, a person pays, in addition to money, with his independence and again we drive the same or a new brand further. Figuratively we can say that in the future, we will have a "full-blooded", "spiritual" life of brands with the participation of consumers who are realized through brands and them. But on the other hand, is there a big difference in the fact that a person idolizes an old, often confusing cultural idea (religion) or a new commercial brand (clear and made for him, as they say, positioned).

Thus, brand owners became powerful new priests, just as economics replaced or supplanted many things which a person from the "good-brand" world with the help of marketing has now translated into a brand.

Let's now outline some modern brand attributes and branding trends:

1)Anthropomorphism, the humanity of brands with their inherent ideal traits and aspirations (the same that a person attributes to everything higher)

2)Quality and reliability are no longer key factors when choosing a brand by a consumer since they are implied by the default required product attributes present in the product

3)Consumers begin to resist "naked" technical attributes and new products without exposing them to an intuitive and aesthetic basis

4)When creating brands, there is a shift from "external" approaches based on such indicators as popularity, demand, uniqueness, etc. to "internal" metrics that take into account consumer perception, analysis of the human perception of a brand, trends in perception of people under the influence of a brand

5)New brands are beginning to insist more and more on what they believe in, and offer consumers to join their faith. They want not only to please the consumer but to convince him of the correctness and uniqueness of their vision of the world, to give the consumer support and confidence.

6)Showing great persistence and sometimes aggressiveness, the brand is trying at any cost to capture the attention of the consumer and not let him go, using the recommendations of psychologists, sociologists, linguists, etc. when creating and implementing your integrated communication with the consumer (both mass and personal)

7)When developing a modern trademark, on the one hand, the portrait of future consumers, the factors that determine their decisions and actions (speak the language of the consumer) are taken into account, and on the other hand, those ideas and values are developed and offered to consumers that they can perceive as their own or as desired, to which they are ready to strive (consumer formation)

## *Future*

The association of brands within one lifestyle concept will be based on the principles of similarity and complementarity between different brands in all product categories, as well as contribution to the creation of an overall viable concept. The creation of several different concepts of lifestyle, unified in the internal style of brands within them, which will provide the entire spectrum and all levels of human needs, as well as his entire life cycle (from birth to death) is no longer a matter of the not so distant future.

This implies significantly higher consumer loyalty and acceptance of the philosophy of this lifestyle at a deep psychological level even in early childhood. In the meantime, before the formation of this monolithic complex of agreed brands.

# CHAPTER 2

## How to Manage Your Brand Identity?

**B**rand management or branding consists of a series of strategies to build a brand, whether personal or belonging to a company. The objective is to create, publicize, reinforce, and maintain a series of values inherent to the company, helping its public identify it. Therefore, this concept includes each of the company's actions and is carried out by the company to become a brand easily recognizable by the public.

Although some marketing agencies distinguish between the branding of a company and that of a brand, the truth is that one cannot be distinguished from the other since any positive or negative perception that either of them reaps will automatically affect the other. For example, more than once, it has happened that a food company that has had to withdraw a particular product from the market has seen sales suffer in others.

### 2.1 Brand Management

Likewise, it should not be overlooked that the brand concept goes much beyond the logo since it also encompasses the attributes, values , and symbols with which the public relates to a company, making it their business card and your most crucial hallmark.

What aspects condition the brand Identity?

The perception that the public has of the brand is subject to numerous variables. Anyway, these are some of the factors that can affect your reputation the most:

1) The coherence between the messages and the real situation. Launching an advertising claim can be a double-edged sword. Although it can add value to the company compared to its competitors (for example, if it claims to be the cheapest option on the market), this can also work against it if this information is not real. The same happens with the benefits and benefits they promise in their products and services (imagine the broadband line).

This factor also affects the brand or company logo, undoubtedly one of the most relevant branding elements.

2) The ability to anticipate and meet user demands. The fact that a brand holds a leadership position does not mean that it can afford not to continue implementing initiatives to improve or, at least, to stay in a prominent place. Having a constant adaptation innovation capacity is an essential tool so that companies do not get left behind concerning the competition. And for that, it is essential to listen to your current and potential customers' needs and know how to adapt to them in the shortest possible time.

3) Your role on social media. This affects the management of the corporate profiles themselves and the messages that other Internet users generate and share. Thus, not regularly updating a brand's page on Facebook, Twitter, or similar platforms (and with quality content), not acting upon a negative comment from third parties either by responding or adopting legal measures, if applicable, no Addressing users' questions and complaints or not having a presence in those social media used by the brand's target audience can seriously damage online reputation.

4) Customer service (and all users). Offering quality service and knowing how to manage and solve user complaints quickly are essential aspects of building and maintaining the right brand identity. Ultimately, it is a strategic issue to which the utmost attention should be paid.

5) Crisis management. Any company, from a small SME to a multinational, can already suffer a brand crisis. Although the reasons can be multiple (from the appearance of a batch of products in poor condition to a smear media campaign due to an issue carried out by the company, for example), the steps that must be followed must be correctly described a crisis protocol. They must include an immediate response (although not for that reason well prepared and thoughtful), direct communication with the affected people and society, and concrete actions to reverse the situation as soon as possible.

Hence, we must not lose sight of the following maxim: "If you don't talk about yourself, others will do it for you."

## 2.2 How to Improve Your Brand Identity?

The data provided provides clues to some actions that can help improve your brand identity:

1) Review and renew the brand identity when appropriate (which affects the logo, signage, etc.). The presentation of a new product line or the inauguration of a new shopping center is usually a perfect occasion since, in this way, the image of the logo will be linked to a positive aspect.

2) Diversify and streamline customer service channels. The rise and multiplication of social networks and instant messaging services (such as WhatsApp or Telegram) have made them another channel of communication for those who want to address the company. It has also caused them to demand more and more immediate attention.

Hence, diversifying the contact channels and reducing response times is a required subject to improve branding.

3) Careful social profiles with relevant content. Various studies, such as the one carried out by e-Interactive on this issue, assure that around 7 out of 10 users prefer to find out about a company for its content rather than for advertising impacts. Thus, it is convenient to disseminate on social networks, and periodically, articles and information of quality and that are useful for the company's target audience.

4) Respond and manage criticism. When a negative comment arises, the company must provide its version as quickly as possible and put the means to solve any problems that it may have caused. Also, for this, social networks are an ally that must not be lost sight of.

## *Take Care of Branding*

### Reasons You Need to Take Care of Your Brand Identity

Given the increase in supply and homogenization of the same in fact, more and more companies offering the same type of products with characteristics almost identical, the branding is the factor that can help a company stand out from other similar brands.

In any case, in the same way that this can become a differentiating factor, it can also turn against the company if it is not appropriately managed (both from an online and offline point of view). For example, poor customer service on social networks or the absence of a content strategy can negatively affect the company.

Thus, it is essential to allocate resources to manage the brand image from a transversal perspective, including corporate communication and social communication. Only in this way can your brand identity be consolidated and maintained, an essential factor for any business activity's success or failure. Without going any further, the brand is what distinguishes an organization from its competitors.

## 2.3 Other Perfect Strategy

Today, the world is evolving in a period of significant social, economic, and technological transformations. The current context is characterized not only by constant change but also by its acceleration. This poses significant challenges for companies and offers excellent opportunities for those who can better interpret and anticipate changes and respond to them more quickly. Consequently, many of the paradigms that worked until recently in brand management have become obsolete. Let's check out 7 paradigm changes in the current management of brands.

### 1. From Product to Brand Management

Differentiation strategies have evolved from an orientation based on the product and its benefits to focusing on the brand and its meanings. This displacement process began more than two decades ago, but the changes in the context and the factors mentioned above have intensified it.

It is increasingly difficult to find differentiation elements based on product attributes and maintain them over time; it is even more so. The brand and its meanings are the compacts of the new differentiation strategies. The big difference is that if before the usual thing was to think about a product, develop it, prepare a marketing plan and in the end, ask yourself: what brand do we put on it? Today the process must be the reverse: first, you have to ask yourself the value essential that inspires your brand? And from this, define the products that conceptually fit into the said territory of meaning.

### 2. From Promises to Experiences in Brand Management

Recently, the experiences that revolve around the product areas or more important than the product itself establish a differentiation on which to base a sustainable competitive advantage.

An efficient way of defining what a brand is as "the promise of an experience." If we understand it this way, its managers must have the capacity and the necessary powers not only to define the promise as I have mentioned before but also to influence the factors that are necessary to guarantee that the promise is fulfilled and that the company is capable of generating the desired experience with your product or service (and everything that surrounds you) in your customers. This requires coordinating many aspects and influencing many elements and people over which brand managers often do not have hierarchical authority, so they must exercise their best skills to influence and involve everyone in the project.

Jeff Bezos, the CEO of Amazon, says companies should reverse the balance between promise and experience. From "overpromise and under-deliver" (which is what most companies do), he suggests moving on to "under-promise and over-deliver."

### 3. From Notoriety to Relevance

Acquiring notoriety has been a priority objective in brand management for decades, and advertising its main instrument. However, in the new context, it is relevant that makes a brand valuable. Consequently, the construction of brands does not depend on the advertising investment capacity but on the ability to achieve relevance among the public of interest. Which can sometimes be more difficult since notoriety is bought, but relevance has to be earned.

A brand is relevant when it connects with the desires, needs, and aspirations of the target audience when it makes life easier for them and is part of their identity as individuals. When continually surprises. When you have a clear and attractive vision and personality, if it disappeared, it would leave a significant gap between its fans (according to some studies, less than a third of the brands would pass this test).

## 4. From Transactions to Relationships

The challenge today is not only to generate transactions but to build and maintain relationships. Therefore, to compete successfully, it is not enough to have a good marketing plan, but also to develop a branding strategy that allows building your brand capable of attracting, generating, and developing links with the public of interest (not only customers!), in a process that begins long before the sale and does not end with it.

Unlike what has been done so far, companies are beginning to put more tremendous efforts into retention to avoid the effect of the "leaky bucket", an expression that refers to the wasted effort and the extra cost involved in prioritizing customer acquisition versus retention, not just for a particular company, but for an entire industry.

## 5. From Commercial Communication to Conversations Around Content

In addition to what has been previously stated at the beginning of this chapter, it is evident, and much has already been said, that communication is no longer one-way and that it is necessary to establish authentic conversations with people (I am reluctant to call them consumers!). This forces companies to have a natural disposition towards dialogue (which is not so common) and a great capacity to listen, which is increasingly being done by companies thanks to the new digital tools that exist for this. Not feeling heard is one of the main reasons why someone changes the brand and partner also by the way;).

The content phenomenon is here to stay; it is not a fad, although as happens with some phenomena that are talked about so much, they wear out before they come of age. Indeed, the concept of "branded content" is still diffuse. Branded content is often used to refer to a camouflaged variant of a viral campaign, product placement, or sponsorship when it is something else. In the first place, what we call branded content should instead be called "people's content" since it is not about talking about what the brand wants but about what people are interested in. Of course, do it according to your brand's identity and purpose, in the key that defines its strategic concept and its personality as a brand.

Through content, brands establish dialogue and build relationships with people, sometimes being the host and other times just another guest. That is why content is a crucial way to build relevance for the brand and associate it with a meaningful territory.

## 6. From Controlling to Co-Managing

Managers must accept that they do not have control of the brand management entirely in their hands. Brands belong to customers and the community as well as to companies, to the point that they have in their hands a decisive capacity for intervention to determine their success or failure. This requires new ways of working through co-management and co-creation systems, that is, of power and shared creation. Heineken, P&G, or Nivea are making essential efforts in co-creation with clients to generate new products.

If companies want to connect with people, they have to be willing to control their brands. People are willing to make brands their own (more than ever), to get involved, to collaborate, but in return, they demand that companies do not disappoint them, that they surprise them, that they take them into account, and of course, that they be honest and authentic.

## 7. From Identity to Culture

Not only, but especially in service companies, it is essential to forecast your brand inward before doing it outward. In relation to what has been said in several of the previous points, causing an experience is the outcome of the job carried out by people. And generating content is a job done by people. So these should be the first to be seduced by the brand and impregnate with its magic.

Zappos is a prominent example. It is one of the five best-valued companies to work for in the USA and has unique practices, such as attracting talent. Those who want to work in the company must access a network in which they interact with the people in the organization, and it is these who decide, or at least decisively influence, whether or not that person is hired. The Zappos brand promise is based on offering exceptional service. And it does, thanks, of course, to the involvement of all the people in your organization, who are positively identified with your brand.

Undoubtedly, the 7 aspects that I have highlighted (which we have seen are closely related) do not reflect everything that is happening. Still, they illustrate the enormous paradigm shift that occurs in the way you must manage your brand identity in the world's new context.

# CHAPTER 3
## Building a Unique Brand Identity

### 3.1 Your Brand Identity Features

The classic definition of a brand describes it as a means of identification and differentiation; therefore, brand identity is a system of characteristics that determines its uniqueness and uniqueness. All brand properties can be divided into three categories.

The first includes the declared features of the brand, i.e., those that are explicitly offered or promised to the consumer, let's call them promises. The second category includes such characteristics that require specific actions (facts) confirming their presence; they can be called confirmation.

The second group of brand features is formed gradually in interactions between the consumer and the brand. The second category includes the brand's character, trust, friendship, and respect for the brand.

The third category includes implied or implicit promises; instead, consumer expectations are how customers would like the brand to be. Expectations are formed from the experience of consumption of goods in this category and the peculiarities of contacts with a particular brand. When developing a brand and its identity, one deals only with promises, i.e., with those characteristics of the brand that apply to potential consumers and how the consumer can identify this brand.

Confirmations are mainly determined by the brand's communicative quality and its ability to maintain contact with the target audience, organize and direct communications, and thus build and strengthen the consumer-brand relationship. Expectations are most important at studying consumer perception of a brand since the difference between what is proposed and expected can significantly distort the brand image and reduce consumer activity.

Promises, given or implied by manufacturers, and consumer expectations are essential characteristics that define your brand. Therefore, Philip Kotler called a successful brand "the promise of the seller to constantly provide its customers with a specific set of qualities, benefits and services." University of London marketers Paul Smith, Chris Berry, and Alan Pulford have defined branding as "the language of consumer expectations."

Sometimes the description of competitive brands as a person is used to define brand identity. Consumers describe a brand as a set of human qualities. Various projective techniques allow us to identify and metaphorically describe the main differences between competing brands. One such method was developed by advertising agency Bates and is called the Brand Wheel.

## 3.2 Brand Values

Developing a brand identity involves defining the values that a given brand symbolizes and which the consumer is ready to join.

These are the values that support his ideas about his personality and his position in society. Therefore, it is advisable to divide values into individual and social. The values that define the brand must be relevant to the target group; otherwise, consumers will not react. In other words, the values should be precious. On the other hand, the values themselves or their combination must be specific and, if possible, unique so that this value system does not resemble the essential qualities of other brands from the same or related product group. Brand values should emphasize its individuality and not turn the brand into a "common place."

What values should the brand bring to the masses?

Those that most fully and accurately characterize the target consumer group. In this regard, the brand is similar to the club of the same name since a real brand unites a group of people who have chosen it. If a brand is positioned in terms of values, it proclaims them with conviction and passion; it becomes a symbol, or a cultural code, expressing both the values themselves and the consumers for whom these values are significant. People who are loyal to your brand have standard features. The main task of branding is to capture and express these features so vividly and thoroughly that the given brand becomes a symbol of consumer unification. And then the brand will become a "club" that has gathered such people.

David Aaker points to five components of brand value:

1. Consumer awareness of the brand.

2. Consumer perception of quality and reputation.

3. Brand associations.

4. Loyalty of consumers to the brand.

5. Other patented brand values (trademarks, patents, know-how, etc.).

Consumers prefer high-value brands because they find it easier to recognize and understand the brand's benefits, they feel more trust in it, and they get more profound satisfaction from using the product. Manufacturers prefer more valuable brands, as such brands create consumer loyalty to their brand, which allows them to sell goods at higher prices, makes it possible to stretch and expand the brand and stimulates the effectiveness of marketing programs.

"Anyone can start a business, but it takes genius, faith and true enthusiasm to create a brand," said famous brand connoisseur David Ogilvy. Today's consumer market is a battleground for goods and services for a place in the sun, driven by brand advertising and brand building.

The concept of a brand is broader than a trademark since it additionally includes:

- the product or service itself with all its characteristics;
- a set of characteristics, expectations, associations perceived by the user and attributed to the product (product image, brand-image);
- information about the consumer;
- promises of any benefits given by the brand's author to consumers;

Hence, the creators themselves put into it (a fairly common mistake is that brand creators believe that their perception and the perception of the target audience are the same; in practice, they quite often differ from the perception of the consumer).

At any given moment, any brand has a particular Brand Image: a unique set of associations that are now in the minds of consumers. These associations express what the brand stands for right now, and there is a momentary promise to consumers from the creators of the brand.

Any new product that appears on the market creates a particular impression on the consumer. Sometimes positive, sometimes negative. The first impression is usually the strongest. In particular, an advertising campaign can shape a brand image. It is important to note that brand image is what is in consumers' minds now, whereas brand identity is a much longer-term concept.

There are two approaches to shaping customer experience: spontaneous and controlled. The product is at a disadvantage with a spontaneous approach: buyers may not see its possible advantages, not appreciate the advantages, and exaggerate the disadvantages.

The controlled approach initially implies selecting a given product from a group of similar ones by presenting it in a favorable light and focusing on its merits.

This approach is nothing more than branding.

In addition to the previously provided definition, branding is creating and managing a brand, which includes advertising activities, the primary purpose of which is to form a specific image of the advertised brand, company, product, and service in the consumer.

The brand has the following characteristics:

1) Brand Attributes: the main associations that buyers (clients) have when they perceive a brand. They can be both positive and negative; they have a different degree of importance for the buyer and his satisfaction for different market segments.

2) The brand (Brand Essence): the most striking characteristic, the idea of the brand, the decisive argument for the consumer's choice of this brand.

3) Brand identity (Brand Identity): a set of all characteristics that form the brand's uniqueness. The personality of a brand expresses what sets it apart from other brands.

4) Brand Image is a momentary unique associative array formed in the imagination of the consumer. A brand image can be shaped by an advertising campaign carried out by the media.

However, when launching a new electronic brand on the market, it is necessary to consider some distinctive features due to the peculiarities of the new communication environment, which is the Internet.

The same brand affects different consumers differently. This allowed creating a particular hierarchy of image (impression), the starting point of which is complete distrust of the brand, and the upper limit is exceptional loyalty.

A negative image is the worst thing that can happen to a brand. It causes only negative emotions in consumers.

Lack of awareness: such a brand is possessed, for example, by newly formed companies.

Brand awareness: for example, you know that there are different brands of clothing, but this does not mean that you prefer one of them or even wear.

Brand preference: for example, preferring to wear classic clothes.

Loyalty to a brand is a sign of exceptional loyalty to that brand. At the same time, the consumer is not at all obliged to be aware of this attachment.

## 3.3 Opportunities

New technical opportunities that have emerged in recent years, especially the proliferation of the Internet and the emergence of e-commerce, make their adjustments to how businesses operate, how consumers make decisions and shop, and how a successful brand is built. The global network opened up the broadest horizons of choice for buyers, provided suppliers with additional chances to sell their products, and, therefore, created new marketing competition segments and set brand managers more difficult tasks of forming market symbols, traditions, patterns, ideals, and myths in society.

Compared to the offline business environment, new markets are much more likely to emerge on the Internet. Also, there is a continuous process of changing old markets, new niches and business opportunities are emerging. This process is going very quickly; in each segment, there is a fierce struggle for users, customers, image, that is, for a place in the market. The Internet is a unique medium, thanks to which it is possible to obtain precise data on the consumer's attitude to the brand in real-time to build a system of visitors' preferences. Conversely, the consumer himself can recognize the "objective" components of the brand without wasting time.

An Internet brand (e-brand) is a set of characteristics of a product/service defined by the following parameters:

- the sufficiency of the informative content of the website and the correct tone of dialogue with the consumer;
- the personification of advertising messages to a specific consumer, depending on his social and demographic portrait;
- a high degree of usability of the Internet resource.

Usability is the efficiency, and productivity of any activity tool.

For an online store, the most critical usability properties are ease of access to the necessary information for the target audience and predefined scenarios for the paths of individuals from different segments of the target audience. Usability is determined based on focus group research data and characterizes the convenience and simplicity of working with an electronic store.

Absolute confidentiality of information about site visitors (about buyers of electronic stores). In the United States, civil society organizations provide this degree of consumer protection. In some other parts of the world, everything is still based on consumer confidence in a particular electronic store.

Security of monetary transactions. This problem is not very relevant for developed countries because less than 20% of payments are made online (i.e., by credit card through various Internet payment systems).

As an entrepreneur, you enter the market with a strong product or service. For you, this is an idea, a unique concept that meets a need, and above all, that has a lot to offer. But bringing that product or service, however useful and relevant it may be, to the market is not enough. In an extremely competitive environment, where consumers are inundated with messages, content, proposals, promises, and incentives, you will have to show yourself, sell yourself, and above all, get out of the game by building a strong brand.

It is indeed by creating a strong brand with its universe and a unique promise that you will make you outstanding from the crowd and attract your target audience's attention. But what exactly is the definition of a strong brand? A strong brand is a brand whose personality, codes, and values enter the consumer's daily life to make a lasting place there. It is a brand that is part of "furniture", so much does it become an object of life and everyday life, such as a jar of Nutella or a bottle of Coca Cola!

But it's not Ferrero or Coca who wants, so how can you also make your brand a strong brand? Well, we have some simple tips for you:

**1 Give Your Brand a Personality**

Ask yourself who you are and what you do. Then define your mission to your consumers and the promise you make to them as a brand. This work, which may seem tedious and necessary, is the foundation of your brand universe's entire construction, the axis of differentiation compared to your competitors, and the clarity of your message to the public. From there, determine how you will communicate it: what tone to use, what words, what values. Ask yourself: if my brand was someone, what kind of person would it be?

## 2 Understand Your Audience and Live for Them

Understanding who it is for is the key to a strong brand. Who are your customers, and what do they want from you? Study them with surveys, focus groups, and analyze their behavior on social networks: what do they react to, what do they like, for what reasons do they get involved? What sites do they visit, what purchases do they make, and how? When you understand what they are likely to like the most about your products and materials, make your communication reflect every element.

## 3 Identify Your Core Target and Stick to It

The priority is your target audience: don't try to please everyone. Be precise and concise by getting straight to the point. Many small businesses have failed by communicating too broadly from the start. Initially, you address a niche: identify it, stick with it, and don't change your fundamental promise. Examples include Air BNB, Uber, Netflix, or Spotify, which started by communicating with a niche target before becoming global brands, which became "strong brands."

## 4 Be Consistent

Your brand universe must be identifiable everywhere, on all your media and in all your speaking engagements. Whether it's your logo, website, business cards, flyers, social networks, POS, everything must match, be done in the same tone, and the same graphic and editorial lines. To not get lost along the way, you can quickly set up a graphic and editorial charter allowing all members of your company and your partners to express themselves consistently.

## 5 Grow with Your Audience.

Communication and image technologies evolve too quickly, and consumers change habits just as quickly. Don't miss the mark and don't rest on your laurels: be always on the lookout for how your competitors speak up, pay attention to how your consumers interact on social networks and your website, stay informed of the latest trends in digital marketing and be at the forefront of innovation in the tools that allow a brand to stay on-trend. With this, you can build a formidable and unique brand identity.

# CHAPTER 4

## Your Brand Identity Marketing Analysis

As previously stated in the last chapter, I'd love to expatiate more on marketing analysis to build your brand identity correctly. Remember, marketing activity begins with an analysis of the market situation; to get an initial idea of which it is necessary to formulate answers to four questions.

### *4.1 The Four Questions*

**1. Where Are We?** The answer to this question implies the creation of a spatial model expressing where the company, the product it produces, competing companies with similar products, products of a higher price category, substitute products, as well as the main groups of consumers located and moving in this "semantic space." Such a model allows one to describe the dynamics of the market (features of positioning and consumer perception of each brand), as well as those significant variables that accelerate or slow down these processes, "pulling" consumers to semantic dominants or "pushing them away."

**2. Where Do We Want to Be?** This is the destination (goal) of the brand in the semantic space for the coming years. The second question's answer is to describe the brand's planned location in terms of such a space of values as consumers should perceive it.

**3. What Is Needed to Appear There?** When answering this question, one must consider the current situation and the prospects for its development: production capacity, financial capabilities and investments, experience and qualifications of personnel, the time factor, etc.

**4. What Can Hinder the Atom?** Here it is essential to take into account market dynamics ( market capacity, its expansion or contraction), changes in macroeconomic situations (incomes of the population, inflation rates, exchange rates, prices for raw materials and energy resources, etc.), the possible activity of competitors, changes in consumer perception, obsolescence and the emergence of new models, the dynamics of fashion and consumer tastes, as well as government regulation (laws, taxes, licensing, customs duties, etc.).

By answering these four questions and describing the marketing situation as a spatial model, you can visualize where your brand is among the competitive brands, what market prospects it has, and what direction it should develop. In addition, describing the position and dynamics of brands in the most appropriate categories for this situation helps identify the key concepts that determine the market's development. These semantic determinants are decisive for the description of the brand and its identity. SWOT analysis allows you to answer the third and fourth questions in the form of a division of the required resources and possible restrictions.

## *4.2 SWOT Analysis*

In SWOT analysis of the company's activities, all factors are divided into two directions: wealth/deficiency of internal resources (Strength - strength; Weakness - weakness) and favorable / limiting external factors (Opportunity - opportunities; Threat - threats). Usually, SWOT analysis is carried out in the form of a table.

SWOT analysis allows, by comparing development opportunities with limitations, to work out an optimal strategy for the company's development, making the most positive aspects and compensating for the constraining factors.

## Analysis of Manufactured Goods

In marketing, a product is any product of a manufacturer's activity designed to satisfy a desire or need. A product is an object of consumption. Therefore, the analysis of manufactured products concerns a set of issues affecting various aspects of this product's consumption. First of all, what is the product intended for, what needs or desires it satisfies, its function, the quality and reliability of the product, the benefits and benefits for the consumer from its use, and much more.

## Appointment of Goods:

This section covers a range of issues related to the value of a given product, its function, everything for which it is intended, and how it implements its purpose. Those desires or needs determine the purpose of a product that it can satisfy and the instability or shortage of something important that the consumer replenishes with this particular product's help.

## Product Quality:

The concept of "quality" expresses a set of features that determine a particular object or phenomenon. Since the product is intended for consumption, its quality is determined by the ability to perform its functions to satisfy customers' desires or needs. There are two aspects of product quality: from the standpoint of producers and the standpoint of consumers. "Quality of a manufacturer" is a set of properties of a product designed, manufactured, and offered to customers. "Consumer quality" is defined by how consumers perceive a product's quality, what they pay attention to when buying and using it. Consumer quality depends on the social stratum of buyers, their opinions, experience, and mass perceptions that determine the quality and differences of various brands of goods in consumers' minds.

The qualities of the producer and the consumer can differ significantly from each other. For example, high-quality (from the manufacturer's point of view) socks once made were not in demand among consumers. As it turned out, customers, having a habit of touching the material with their fingers before buying it, did not have this opportunity since these socks were wrapped entirely in transparent polyethylene. When they began to make a "window" in the packaging of socks, sales increased sharply. When developing and developing a brand, the product's functional quality is of great importance and quality by consumers.

**Product Reliability:**

One of the most critical aspects of a product's quality is its reliability, which is the ability of the product to fulfill its purpose in the event of unfavorable external influences. There are four aspects of reliability.

- Reliability: the ability of a product to maintain basic quality parameters during operation.
- Durability is the ability to fulfill its purpose for a specified period.
- Safety is the ability to withstand factors that worsen the physical and mental health of the consumer.
- Maintainability is the ability to restore its purpose after failure.

**Benefit for The Consumer:**

The purpose of the product from the manufacturer's point of view and the purpose of the product from the point of view of the consumer may also differ. This difference is often formulated as the difference between what is sold (offered to the buyer) and what is bought (what the consumer needs). This difference is precisely noted in the

43

American proverb: "They sell drills, but they buy holes of the required diameter." Consumer perception of the purpose and quality of a product lies in the concept of its usefulness.

The benefits of using a particular brand of the product can be different for different segments of the population. This allows the segmenting of consumers for the desired benefit. For example, R. R. J. Haley divided the core of toothpaste consumers into four categories depending on the kind obtained benefits: the taste and appearance of the product, the whiteness of the teeth, preventing illness teeth price.

Benefits can be seen as "gain", it is close to the concept of efficiency. The benefit is understood as getting the maximum result at the lowest cost (money, time, etc.). Benefits and especially benefits assessed by consumers imply comparing a given brand with similar products; this comparison between adjacent brands is highlighted in a separate section, "Competitive Analysis".

Analysis of the manufactured product, its purpose, quality, benefits, and benefits for consumers allows us to form an accurate position for the brand, an integral part of the brand identity.

## 4.3 Competitive Analysis

There are many excellent marketing books devoted to different aspects of market research, so here is just a shortlist of competitive analysis's central areas. First, the product group's main characteristics are described, which includes the brand you are interested in; then, it is necessary to study the peculiarities of related product groups, from where manufacturers and new brands can come to the current market.

This analysis is performed separately for each of the five price categories (low - end, low, middle, high, high - end), while competitors from the nearest price segments are of the most significant interest. Particular attention should be paid to substitute goods since, in the event of a worsening economic situation and a decrease in income, consumers may switch to such brands of goods. The object of marketing research is searching for unfilled market niches, studying their capacity, and factors affecting consumption volumes.

## 4.4. Customer Segmentation

Whereas competitive analysis provides insight into the supply market, the demand market's study begins with segmenting consumers. In 1956, W. Smith put forward the idea that the demand for goods depends not only on the level of competition and prices but also on differences between users. Thus, the first steps were taken towards what is now called segmentation, i.e., dividing consumers into homogeneous groups, in each of which they equally understand the purpose of the product and the benefits from its use.

Therefore, consumers of such a group can be influenced by the same means of marketing communications. The basis for segmentation can be consumer characteristics, lifestyle, consumption volumes, brand loyalty, sought benefits, reasons for making a purchase, etc. The type of segmentation is determined by the specifics of the market and product specifics. Thus, the following basis for segmentation depending on the commodity group:

Segmentation can be divided into three main areas: geography, demography, and psychograph.

**Geographic Segmentation:**

This way of dividing consumers is expressed in defining the market's territorial boundaries, within which consumers are a homogeneous layer. Distinguish between regional, national, international, multinational, and global markets. Geographic segmentation can be

45

carried out by the place of residence of consumers, by the place of purchase, by the place of use of the product, etc.

**Socio-Demographic Segmentation:**

This is the most common way to separate consumers. To define a homogeneous group, customers are segmented by sex and age, marital status and family size, education, occupation, social status, and income. Modern studies also include religion, political preferences, nationality, culture, and language of communication.

**Psychographic Segmentation:**

This division is based on the psychological characteristics, life values, and lifestyles of consumers. They are identified in different groups based on social values: "researchers," "social registrar," "experimenter," "main consumer," "belonging to a certain class," "Survivor," and "man without a goal."

Using the VALS techniques ( the Values And LifeStyles: values and lifestyles) divided American Sgiach consumers into nine classes:

- integral (2%),
- achieved success (20%),
- imitators (10 %),
- socially minded (11%),
- empiricists (5%),
- self-oriented (3%),
- belonging to a certain class (38%),
- maintaining their existence (7%)
- and surviving (4%).

Thus, psychographic studies are varied. In some of them, the names very eloquently characterize the typical representatives of a particular group. The group names speak for themselves, but for clarity, here are two more detailed descriptions.

Gorgeous and dazzling: These are rich women, very fashionable, they buy only the best. They are active shoppers, actively involved in society, using their social life for their careers. When they are picky about their appearance, they rest actively, but not energetically. They spend their holidays in exotic locations.

Bullseye and beer belly: They are big old bumps: lazy from work, like the simple life and regular drinking in the pub. Tabloid readers and arm-wrestling fans.

In the last two or three years, the description of social classes and consumers' segmentation by belonging to one class or another have become popular in some part of the world. Psychographic segmentation holds excellent promise for branding practice. It allows a detailed study of life values and an orientation towards respecting consumers loyal to a particular brand, to use this information for accurate and useful marketing communications.

Ultimately, brand building and development activities begin with traditional marketing activities. SWOT analysis allows you to identify external factors and internal resources that affect the company's activities and the goods it produces. The study of the manufactured product consists of determining its purpose, and the desires or needs that it satisfies, the quality and reliability of the product produced, the benefits, and benefits that its use gives.

The analysis of competitive brands of one product group in all price categories and the study of market capacity, factors influencing its development, is carried out in the "competitive block" of marketing activities. Segmentation of consumers by geographic, socio-demographic, or psychographic principle makes it possible to single out the target group of consumers on which the brand's marketing communications will be oriented.

## Brand Comparisons and Advantages

The foremost step in the practice of branding is to provide a brand identity (brand identity). The very concept of identification presupposes an object's recognition by a set of attributes that define it. Under the brand identity refers to a unique set of features by which users identify this brand. Moreover, these signs can be both material (felt) and meaningful (associations, relationships, benefits, promises, etc.). To "form" a brand in the consumer's mind in the form of a set of interrelated attributes and properties, it is the necessary neck of twist that will determine this particular brand among the many competing brands.

Brand development activities can be divided into two main parts; the first fits into the concept of strategic marketing and consists of identifying significant differences between the brand and competitive brands, correctly selected comparisons that allow consumers to distinguish the brand from the general range, brand positioning and the formation of its concept. The second stage is the development of brand identity, which is how consumers should perceive the brand.

# CHAPTER 5

## Understanding Brand Differences

For the consumer to distinguish a brand among analogs, you must clearly understand how this brand differs from other brands. Brand features can be perceived by our sight, hearing, touch, smell, or taste; such differences are felt. These include size, weight, shape, design, color, smell, taste, softness, etc.

The perceived differences between brands are most comfortable addressing communications, as such differences cannot be denied. For example, there is more toothpaste in a tube than in a standard package; the presence of bubbles in the chocolate or the thermal mark on the beer label. It is rather difficult to refer to taste or smell since these sensations are subjective, and, as you know, "there is no comrade for taste and color."

Imperceptible differences objectively exist, but either is inaccessible to direct perception or is difficult to distinguish. Imperceptible differences include the car's stability, the uninterrupted computer, the durability of household appliances, etc. This category of brand distinctions also includes technical support and advice in technically complex goods, warranty, and additional services.

Advertising often uses special techniques to translate subtle differences into perceived ones, making the benefits of a brand more visible. The ad for Fairy dishwashing detergent features a variety of clean dishes, and Ariel's laundry detergent features white shirts washed with regular powder.

What should a brand do that does not have any significant differences?

It remains only to invent them and declare: "Mark A is the only one, since it has B." Imagined differences are usually born in marketing departments or ad agencies and only exist in marketing communications. It is often tough to grasp the line between imperceptible or imaginary differences, and the consumer can only guess whether xylitol exists in chewing gum, ceramides - in shampoo, bifid bacteria - in yogurt, vita-Calpin - in waffles, Vitavite - in detergent or a layer of drive-wave in sanitary napkins.

## 5.1 Comparisons

Informing the consumer about the differences in your brand needs to be compared with something. If in your messages you do not compare your product with a competitive product, product category, etc., then the consumer will do it himself, comparing the information received with what he knows about similar products. The result of such a comparison is beyond the control of the manufacturers and may not be in favor of your brand. Therefore, it is so important to compare your product in such a way as to show more vital and more convincingly those noticeable differences and significant advantages that distinguish your brand from the available row. Such comparisons are very different, and not all of them are accurate and correct.

**Direct Comparison:**

In countries where comparative advertising is not prohibited, competing brands are often compared. An example of an open comparison of competitive brands in the following ad: an eight-year-old boy buys a can of Coca-Cola from a street vending machine and puts it on the asphalt, then he buys a can of Pepsi, which he places next to Coca. After that, he stands with his feet on these two cans to reach the top button labeled " RC - Cola " and many more.

**Average Product:**

In many countries, direct comparisons require objective and documentary evidence or are generally prohibited. These legal constraints have led to comparisons with a generic product in a given product category. Many are familiar with the expressions "regular battery," "regular toothbrush," or "regular detergent," which are complemented by the display of an average packaging devoid of distinctive features.

This technique like to use the brands of the company Procter & Gamble: " Fairy, the Comet, Ariel, etc. Washing powder washes and as you know, but for less money, and "batteries Duracell; may replace up to ten conventional batteries.

This technique's popularity has led to the appearance of a washing powder "Usual Powder": the savings in advertising funds are evident, but the effectiveness of such a marketing solution and the possibility of developing this brand is highly questionable. What, by and large, can the most common powder in ordinary packaging offer? Probably; just the price. Also, all comparisons of brands with conventional powder are not in favor of the latter.

**Comparison with The Outdated Model:**

This method involves comparing the brand with a previous generation product or with a replacement product. Typically, such comparisons occur in two cases. First, when a fundamentally new revolutionary product enters the market. In the second case, the comparison with a product that has gone out of use (or is out of use) is because the new brand does not differ significantly from its counterparts. Still, against the background of the antediluvian and bulky predecessor, it looks relatively modern and original.

51

Thus, the modern female tampon is compared with the ancient Egyptian "model" made of papyrus. The laser hair removal method is opposed by the removal of unwanted hair with a strip of paper and wax.

**Product Category:**

There is also a comparison with a whole product category; as a rule, these are related product groups, similar in purpose but offering different benefits. For example, women's pads are continually comparing themselves to tampons and antiperspirant rolls to solid deodorants. A typical example of comparison with a whole class of goods is the 7 UP cold drink motto: "No cola!".

**Artificial Comparison:**

This class combines comparisons of a brand with a group of products that it is not entirely correct to compare. For example, lactic Noah soufflé " Milky Way is compared not with the other soufflés and milk "Milk is doubly tasty if it" Milky Way "; Orbit chewing gum compares not with another gum, but with dental protection: " Orbit is the most delicious protection against caries."

Likewise, the safety of a Ford Mondeo is compared to professional security, but not to another reliable car like a Volvo. Here's how it sounds: "Taking care of their safety, some hire professional security, while others buy a new " Ford Mondeo. " Sometimes, artificial comparison can move from manipulating the consumer to the category of metaphor, expanding the initial ideas about the brand, and introducing poetry into the product.

**Comparison with What Is Kept Silent:**

This is a reasonably common technique: the words "better," "more," "faster," "better," implicitly means "in comparison with a similar product." For example, the advertising motto of the "Fairy" brand:

"Copes with greasy dishes better than others" or " Comet ": "Cleanses what others cannot do." The good thing about the method of comparison with the silent is that the analogies are quite understandable. At the same time, the attentive consumer will be able to note the correctness and delicacy of competing companies' products.

**Comparison with Oneself (Zero Positioning Degree):**

The last class of comparisons artificially makes the brand of a product unique, one of a kind. For example, the coffee "Nescafe Gold" is compared to itself: "The one and only. Divine scent. Alluring taste. Delightful memories. Enjoying perfection does not require words. Silence is evil. Nescafé Gold: Striving for Excellence". Or, even more clearly: Orbit "the only chewing pads with quality " by Orbit, "Cigarettes" Peter I of ": always first!" Comparison with oneself gives consumers the impression that only this brand of goods is real; it is unique, making this technique related to the concepts of unique selling proposition and positioning, which we will talk about later.

## 5.2 Brand Benefits

A comparative context is needed to state that a given brand is better than others. Thus, buyers' attention is focused on those critical and relevant advantages when using this particular brand.

Many brands use core strengths as the core of their marketing communications. Difference-comparison- the advantage is prevalent in advertising. Convincingly, it is enough to recall several well-known slogans: "It costs like one package, and bleaches almost 4 times more" ("Ace"); "We try harder than others" (Avis); "Champion in cleaning and disinfection" ("Domestos"); Better Things for a Better Life (Dupont); "The most economical dishwashing detergent" (" Fairy "); "We bring good things to life" (" GE "); " Gillette - no better for a man!"; "Maximum purity and whiteness" ("Gloss"); "From Paris to Nakhodka" OmSa "the best tights"; "All the best in Brazil is called Pele " and many others.

# CHAPTER 6

## Perception of Quality

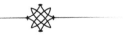

### *6.1 Product Category*

Let us remind you that each product category has specific quality criteria. So, a good eraser should be easy to wash, and a quality condom should be abrasion-resistant. Children's toys cannot have sharp parts, which cannot be said about knives or scissors, where the sharpness and strength of the material determine their quality. Of course, the quality of a product is an essential factor that largely shapes consumer choice. Moreover, it should be noted that the understanding of quality by the manufacturer and the consumer may not only not coincide but even differ significantly from each other.

From the manufacturer's perspective, quality is determined primarily by those regulatory documents that must comply with the product manufactured for sale. These include various standards, technical specifications, laws (for example, the Law on Consumer Rights Protection), and other documents governing the production, storage, distribution, use, and service. The manufactured product must be efficient, safe, and durable; it must be repaired, warranted, or serviced.

It is vital to make a high-quality product, but it is even more critical that consumers perceive a product as good quality. Consumer perception of quality is not determined by the level of technology, manufacturing method, or regulations. Consumer experience, knowledge about the product and its use, and those mass perceptions that compensate for the lack of personal experience and knowledge play a decisive role here. The consumer quality of a brand is associated with interaction with it at all stages (search, selection, purchase, use, after-sales service, etc.) and the ideal result as the consumer sees it.

Studying consumer activity, and in particular, how they perceive quality, can provide valuable material for brand development and positioning. For example, surveys have shown that consumers identify the following quality characteristics (in order of importance) in toothpaste: protects against caries, whitens teeth, freshens breath, tastes good, has natural ingredients, and uses advanced technologies. The cleanliness and whiteness of teeth (from the point of view of consumers) largely determines toothpaste's effectiveness and quality. The vast majority of pastes are white, and boxes and tubes use white and blue (teeth whiteness and cleanliness). What happens if you release a bright red toothpaste? Most likely, buyers will say, "She's too active and destroys my teeth."

The critical quality characteristics perceived by alcohol consumers are purity (transparency), country of origin, and production tradition. Skillful use of the peculiarities of perception and mass representation of consumers allowed the Absolut brand in just five years to gain a leading position in the imported elite alcohol market in the USA.

Two more examples. In 1880, Unilever launched a new ointment under the brand name " Vaseline. " Consumers believed that a high-quality ointment should be transparent, but rather greasy: transparency was associated with cleanliness, and its thickness made the ointment not very liquid, but not too sticky. The new " Vaseline, "which met these requirements, became so popular that the brand name began to be called a whole product category - petroleum jelly over time.

Consumers are convinced that a high-quality condom must be strong enough not to tear but thin and gentle enough not to lose sensation. Any manufacturer who can convince consumers of the exceptional strength and subtlety will have significant advantages over their competitors. It is no coincidence that one of the leading brands is called " Durex "; the morphology of this word: durable + latex ("strong, reliable elastic band"). The manufacturers managed to convey the product category and the main attribute of quality in the name itself. Therefore, every time he hears the name " Durex, "the consumer recalls this purpose and quality of this brand.

In recent years, the very concept of a brand for many consumers has become associated with a high-quality product. Consumer stereotypes and prejudices, mass perceptions, and consumer habits can significantly reduce quality perceptions and discourage individual brands and entire product categories. For example, it is widely believed that many products remain unused in a plastic pyramid bag. Therefore, Maggi mayonnaise in such a package successfully combats this prejudice with the slogan: "Amazingly, every last drop is squeezed out."

The popular belief that a powerful water pipe cleaner can corrode water pipes is a significant deterrent to consuming this product category.

What consumer stereotypes can limit the consumption of herbal tea? Fear that these herbs are harvested in an environmentally unfriendly area, and the herbal collection may contain dangerous microorganisms. Therefore, herbal tea packaging is decorated with a large inscription: "All products have passed microbiological and radiation control." This eliminates possible fears and prejudices that can significantly restrict the use of the product.

## 6.2 Brand Associations

When consumers see the packaging of a product or its advertisement, hear its name, they have a variety of associations. Associations evoked by the brand in the consumer, we call brand associations. These images, feelings, and ideas arise when he perceives one or more brand attributes. Images can be relatively product-independent, where the product or name resembles something, advertised or influenced by consumer experience. Associations brands also include implicit and connotative content of the messages coming from the brand. The first category includes various hints, contexts, subtexts, and double meanings. The second group includes symbolic, emotional, or evaluative messages that convey the consumer's attitude.

There are three levels at which the brand's associative space is developed: relationships, culture, and mythology. The first level of associations is associated with the brand's content, functional, individual, social, and communicative qualities.

**Brand Culture:** When a brand touches on the traditions, customs, and mores of a people, they inevitably fall into its cultural space. A brand that skillfully uses cultural associations is imbued with the people's spirit, becomes a real national treasure, and genuine national pride, an integral part of the culture. For example, it isn't easy to imagine modern Germany without Volkswagen, the BMW, the Audi, Opel, and the Mercedes. Mobile telephones such as the Nokia are the pride of the north's small people, conquered not only the whole of Europe, and even America.

Besides, creating productive and positive associations that use people's cultural perceptions and create an internal mythological space is the most difficult in branding. This chapter will restrict ourselves to only a basic understanding of the brand's culture and mythology and take a closer look at the brand associations associated with its relationship with consumers. These associations can be categorized according to the associated brand characteristics. These are the top brand features supported associatively:

- purpose, product category;
- product quality;
- benefits and advantages;
- country of origin of the brand;
- manufacturer's characteristics;
- consumer characteristics;
- situation of using the goods, etc.

To enable the consumer to evaluate the product's quality for himself, they often focus on the most critical attributes of quality. One of the main requirements for semi-finished products (in addition to taste) is the preparation speed. A country is often associated with a higher standard of living and a higher quality of goods. In this case, hints at the country are used, images of the Eiffel Tower, the Statue of Liberty, or a subtropical beach are used. Famous words are written in Latin script also imply the origin of the goods. For example, the Burger brand alludes to wealthy German residents by its name.

## 6.3 Brand Identity

A strong brand promises and provides quality assurance and offers a means of identification and differentiation. This is the essence of the commercial success of Renault's automotive brand. It provides consumers with an open mind, non-conformists who value practicality, the car's vision, and courage and sincerity. The proposal is designed to support its growth and internationalization policies.

**Positioning concept:** To satisfy consumers without preconceptions, non-conformists, Renault is a dreamy, bold, and warm-hearted car manufacturer that offers to experience the unique pleasure of driving and living in the cabin.

## The Need for Brand Identity

People's perception of the Renault brand varies significantly depending on the geographic region. Often the products themselves have a better image than the brand itself. Without the backing of a strong brand, a product loses most of its appeal, no matter how good it is. A strong brand provides added value to a product, convinces it, makes consumer choice easier, and increases brand loyalty. However, it is equally essential that a strong brand is a source of income for its shareholders.

Renault products are increasingly recognized as having superior conceptual and fundamental qualities. To support its growth and internationalization strategy, these products must be supported by strong brand identity.

## Who are Renault consumers? What is Renault?

The definition given in this guide expresses the company's philosophy and the essence of the brand. " Renault " able to determine the identity of the consumer, "consumers without prejudice non-conformists appreciating practicality." "Renault" defines itself as a "visionary, bold and hearty."

Dreamy, Bold, Hearty. Thus, Renault wishes to express his reverie and courage with enthusiasm and passion. Renault offers its customers to experience "the unique pleasure of movement and life in the cabin." The brand communicates further development of the car-for-life concept, adding a notion of gratitude for the proven pleasure of driving simplicity and car performance.

# CHAPTER 7

## Why Is a Logo as Important as A Brand Identity?

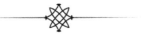

### 7.1 Logo

When a brand wants to assert its identity in the market and be recognized by customers, suppliers, affiliates, users, or the general public, the effort to always give the best side of the logo in the first instance.

The logo is a combination of text or images that serves as the main graphic manifestation of a brand and has the purpose of highlighting its values, differentiating itself from the competition, and attracting consumers.

The first impression is crucial. Sometimes, the only one that counts; this statement may be applied very well in personal relationships, but when it is a company's case, "the first impression" should be taken with caution. Even if a logo is "pretty" or "nice," it is not always the most accurate.

As part of a successful brand identity, appearance of a company, the logo is extremely important because it appears everywhere: on letterhead, on business cards, or in the signature and advertising. It is precisely this that is always and everywhere present for the customer and thus shapes the public's visual appearance.

A logo is essential for the success of an idea. A logo can be used to establish your own identity and serve as a marketing tool. In turn, the more established the logo, the more effective and ambitious presence. That is why the value of a successful logo cannot be given numbers.

Basically, it is about the crowd recognizing the logo and associating something peculiar with it: something special about what is to be presented. For this reason, the philosophy should be conveyed with the logo. The logo is the figurehead. One example is the hype surrounding the Apple brand and its bitten apple, which has long been associated with products and a particular lifestyle.

At best, the logo is distinctive so that people can easily remember it. Various aspects can be taken into account in the design. For example, the meaning of the name of the product or company can be underlined. If it is about a company or a service in general, then the activity can be pointed out. The logo should also address the desired target group. Who should be reached? Also, certain properties, such as product quality, can be in the foreground. It is crucial, however, that the logo evokes associations with the customer.

Hence, a logo's visual aspect must be well thought out and designed according to specific universally accepted parameters. They have the same meaning, such as color and typography, to the brand's visual elements.

**Logo Components**

**Color in The Logo**

Red: It is one of the most popular colors for its power of attraction; it represents passion, emotion, love, vigor and can stimulate the appetite. It is used by many fast-food brands and sports media such as Coca-Cola, KFC, ESPN, Kellog's.

Yellow: It is a warm color that highlights joy, energy, and optimism. Companies like Ferrari, DHL, Shell, and even food and restaurant brands use it in their logos.

Blue: It is associated with stability, confidence, calm, and comfort. It is one of the colors preferred by technology, medical, finance, or automotive companies such as Samsung, IBM, HP, and Ford.

Green: It is usually used to represent harmony with nature and hope. It also highlights life, peace, and growth. Brands like Animal Planet, Lacoste, and Android opt for variations of the green color in their logos.

Purple: Intelligence, creativity, imagination, spirituality are the values that this color highlights, but it is also usually associated with luxury and elegance. Some brands that use it are Hallmark, SYFY, Yahoo!, Wonka.

Black: Symbolizes authority, sophistication, power, and prestige. It is commonly used by brands that want to make it clear that the people who buy their products are select consumers; BlackBerry, Hugo Boss, Nike, Adidas, and BMW are some companies that prefer black for their logos.

Orange: Represents the value of friendship as well as enthusiasm, joy, and delight. Therefore, it is not unusual for brands such as Nickelodeon, Mozilla, Blogger, or Harley Davidson to use this color.

White: Although it is widely used as a companion to other colors or to soften the color palette of a logo, by itself, it symbolizes purity, sobriety, and simplicity. Some brands that prefer to highlight the white color over others are beauty and personal care products.

**Typography in Logos**

With serifs: The serifs are small ornamental lines that are applied at the end of a letter's stroke, imply tradition, heritage. It is ideal for companies that want to emphasize their history.

Without serifs: Without any ornaments, they relate to the straightforward, modernity, stability, and cleanliness. It is used by brand logos to convey a direct and honest message that generates trust in its target.

Italics: Due to their similarity to handwriting, they are considered formal and very decorative. They usually convey creativity, femininity, and elegance. Its use extends a lot in brands that want to highlight their sophistication and spontaneity depending on the elaboration of the line.

Modern: Within the long list of typefaces, modern fonts are a good option because they adapt well to any context. They mix confidence with a touch of class. They are preferred for logos of luxury brands or with a select niche market and exclusive service providers.

New Letters: This section includes all the types of letters that do not fit into the previous ones because they are typical of a specific brand. Their most important characteristic is to emphasize originality; although it is not a rule, many companies use them in the logo without other visual details.

**Hidden Items**

In many cases, brands decide to strategically place detail in their logos that tend to go unnoticed at first glance but which, when found, generates in their clients a certain sensation of brand rediscovery.

Fedex: They promote their speed and precision of delivery through their logo in a special way, with an arrow formed between the "E" and the "X."

Amazon: What stands out in your logo is the arrow that lowered the name of the website. It looks like a soft smile, but the arrow begins at "A" and points to "Z," an indication of the incredible variety of articles they sell to their consumers.

Adidas: There are only three lines that make up the logo of this well-known clothing and sporting goods brand. However, the inclination with which they are arranged symbolizes a mountain and is a metaphor for the challenges athletes must overcome.

The logo evolves with your brand.

As companies succeed in their business, expand, and risk entering other niche markets, the logos representing them also change, especially to adapt to the tastes of the public and new trends in design.

Apple: His first logo was quite elaborate and represented the moment when an apple was about to fall on Isaac Newton's head when he was leaning on the tree. A very detailed drawing that at the end of the 90s changed to a silver-colored bitten apple and has had some simple touches in recent years. A logo that perfectly fits this company wants its products to symbolize: progress, high quality, and cutting-edge technology.

McDonald: The first logos of the popular fast-food chain specified the deliciousness of their products with the word "Famous Barbecue" or even with the drawing of a chef with a hamburger meat face, nowadays the two golden arches that make up the letter "M" are so iconic that nothing else is needed to identify the brand.

Coca-Cola: Since its inception, they have focused on the power of typography. Although the red color is characteristic of this renowned beverage company's containers, the letters that make up the word in white are enough to recognize them immediately.

Nike: One of the best examples of a brand whose logo has evolved over the years to even dispense with the letters of its name to leave as its most iconic image, the well-known "Swoosh," whose central premise is to be synonymous with dynamism.

Together, these cases demonstrate a tendency to go simple but without neglecting the history behind the company. Previously, the marketplace was not so huge and affected by the concept of brand identity that was committed to the same industry or that manufactured the same type of product, so companies could afford to add many details and embellishments to their logos. Still, now the struggle to stand out from competitors can be described as fierce, at least. Hence, brands need to use an instantly identifiable logo, which creates a bond of familiarity with customers.

Nowadays, a logo is an element that distinguishes your company from hundreds of others. Only a unique and exciting logo can be remembered and attract attention to your business. It is he who reflects the essence and specifics of your activity. If you do not have a logo, your name will be lost among competitors, even if you have a fascinating name itself. If there is a logo, but it is outdated, made poorly, etc. this can also lead to very negative consequences because for some clients, this can cause rejection: someone will think that you are not a severe or reputable company.

The logo should speak for itself; it should show how professional and successful you are. We advise you to contact only specialists who will develop and develop something unique, modern, and stylish in logo design.

A logo, which is essentially a trademark, is needed to work in the market. If you decide to do a logo redesign, take this work very seriously. It is essential to consider the pros and cons when you begin this work.

## 7.2 Brand Attributes

So, brand positioning has been carried out; its concept has been developed. It has been determined in which direction the brand should be developed: for whom it is intended, what exactly is offered to consumers, how this product is superior to existing analogs.

The brand identity is then developed and tested with a group of target consumers. The brand's very essence is extracted from the identity. This central idea will run like a red thread through all marketing communications, be contained explicitly, or at least as a hint in all the brand's physical features. Recall that a brand has physical units called brand attributes. The consumer can perceive them directly with the help of the senses. The leading brand attributes are:

- appearance of the product, its physical characteristics;
- brand name;
- packaging;
- advertising;
- brand characters;
- brand name, logo;
- color combinations, corporate fonts;
- gestures touches;
- music, voice, specific phrases;
- natural communicators, etc.

Brand attributes also include any marketing communications related to the brand. These can be advertising images, PR materials, sales promotion events, POS materials, branded shop equipment and display of goods, mail or fax materials, unique appearance and behavior of sellers, enthusiastic customer reviews, and much more. This book deliberately leaves out two crucial brand attributes: appearance, i.e., physical characteristics of the product and advertising. The first category is particular and highly dependent on the product category and competitive peers. Many books, magazines, festivals, and Internet portals are devoted to advertising as marketing communications.

We are primarily interested in those communicators (means of communication) with which a potential consumer most often contacts. It may seem that an essential brand attribute is advertising. Day and void, many brands are familiar to us, mainly through advertising promises. This type of marketing communications is especially crucial at familiarizing with the brand and trial purchases when introducing a new product to the market.

Usually, introductory advertising massively attacks potential buyers' minds for 6-12 weeks, then (after measuring the achieved awareness of the brand among the target audience) its intensity drops several times. What does the consumer face after such an advertising "attack" has ended? Suppose the product belongs to the category of goods bought less than once a month (and this is the majority of all goods). The brand name becomes the primary communicator, and packaging is the second most crucial influencing consumer. For products bought more than once a month, packaging can become the primary means of communication, overshadowing the brand name. Therefore, the description of the brand's attributes starts with the most important with its brand name.

# CHAPTER 8

## Brand Content

If we think about digital marketing as a whole, we will see that it is incredibly dynamic. New methods, techniques, and strategies are increasingly appearing almost routinely around the world. Branded content, despite not being so new, is an extreme example in terms of content production. Understanding what brand content is will give your company more value and provide you with better positioning in the market. Do you want to know more about this great strategy? Keep reading this guide!

Okay, so let's go from the beginning:

### 8.1 What Is Branded Content?

As the name indicates, we can understand it as a strategy to create content directly related to the brand. For the branded content to have the desired effect, the production must be carried out with high quality. Besides that, the content must always be relevant to the audience; it must be objective and appeal to the recipients' emotions.

The change occurs precisely in the disclosure of the brand. If before the public's memory came from advertisements, now it is being formed from the construction of content. Ads today have lost much of their strength with the changing marketplace, so they are often ignored or repudiated.

For this reason, branded content focuses on providing information, entertainment, and fun to your audience. All content is idealized with a concept and a universe of the brand and can be developed in different formats or channels, even as an application.

## How Is Branded Content Made?

Knowing what brand content is can even be a straightforward mission; the most complex part is knowing how to produce it. The two crucial steps for successful development are the surprise effect and relevance, and we will explain why.

In digital marketing, instantaneity is much more accentuated compared to traditional marketing. Actions and reactions must be fast enough not to lose the audience's attention to the competition.

To have the real insight into whether your content is achieving the desired result, you must perform daily monitoring. Only in this way can you identify if the content is generating engagement or interest for your audience.

One of the great secrets of brand content is surprising your audience or provoking their curiosity. When you present a situation that breaks the expectations of your audience, that will undoubtedly generate interest. And, consequently, an increase in potential customers.

The other point refers to relevance. As we mentioned previously, you need to retain the attention of your audience. And producing relevant content is an essential point; the people who will have contact with your production will be responsible for dissemination. If the information is not relevant, it will quickly lose visibility.

Suppose TV ads could reach a large part of the audience, which changes a bit on social media. The first people who have contacted will be the followers of digital platforms. You need to conquer and surprise them to motivate them to share your content. And with that, you can get new points of view and new leads for your page.

**What Is Branded Content for?**

The main objective of brand content is not correctly linked to the sale of products but rather to the brand's positioning in the market. Marketing work is closely linked to building the image and identifying the client with the brand. It is hard work, and it can take several paths, but it is essential for the business.

When working with branded content, you are developing the concept of the brand. More and more consumers are looking for good experiences with companies and getting to know them thoroughly, which has become part of the process. It is much easier for a person to buy a product from a company they already know and are familiar with, where they have gone through a process of approximation and have already earned their trust.

In this way, branded content aims to create an affinity for the company's mission, history, or content. Call the audience and invite them to remember the brand. The sale will be a consequence of the success of the process developed.

Positively this will promote higher sales and greater brand loyalty. Disclosure among friends and family will be an organic consequence. For the person who identifies with that concept, don't be afraid to convey the information clearly and attractively.

Therefore, we can summarize the importance of strategy as follows:

- Strengthen the positioning of the brand in the market;
- Increase brand equity
- Encourage the development of the relationship between the brand and the public;
- Stimulates the emotional, gaining confidence;

- Increase the memory of the brand;
- Create focus and connections.

## What Are the Great Benefits of the Strategy?

Despite being already very present within companies, branded content still causes a lot of interest. Well worth the investment for the results provided. According to content branding experts based on a survey in 2018 on the benefits of production. As a result, they noted the following:

62% of people respond positively to this type of content

67% believe that brand content is more influential compared to other media

17% is the increase in the probability of purchase after applying branded content strategies.

Thinking about bringing relevant and quality content to your followers, you are automatically promoting, creating the best experience for them. You are putting your target audience's needs into consideration, and that is essential for that content to be disseminated later.

### Memory

Surely you should know how important it is to be in the memory of your audience. From the moment you satisfy a person's needs, they will choose your product. When you create an affinity, and it is present in memory, the consumer will actively remember your brand when looking for a product.

### Trust

Maintaining trust and credibility in your brand is key to increasing sales and attracting new customers. It is part of the buying decision process to ensure the brand is trustworthy and building that depends solely on your strategies.

**Mark The Presence**

Understanding brand content is knowing how much presence your brand will have, but without being invasive. Your content will occupy a large proportion of social media channels without having to force anything. Sharing posts, blog articles, videos, podcasts, e-books, or any other format is done naturally because you transmit knowledge and not just sell your product or service!

**Is Branded Content Another Content Marketing?**

This question may have arisen when reading this chapter, and the answer is negative. Branded content has some differences compared to content marketing. However, the strategies are complementary, and both can be used together. The focus should always be aimed at the target audience, promoting the best experience and the most relevant content.

## *8.2 Content Marketing*

Content marketing has become the foundation of inbound marketing for many reasons, but mainly because it has proven to be a very effective way to position a brand. By continually generating and publishing content, brands gain a presence on the Internet and establish a close, interactive, and lasting relationship with their customers and prospects.

This is how content plays an increasingly important role in the process to build and improve your brand image. They are an excellent way to brand, promote, gain credibility, and make your brand stand out from the competition.

## Gain Credibility for Your Brand

Credibility is an aspect that directly affects the image of your brand. That is why you must take care of what you communicate through your content and try to make publications with a specific frequency so that the public does not lose sight of you.

It is imperative to create quality content that is well structured and well-founded. This means that for each content, there must be prior research to have reliable data and sources. The contents that meet these basic requirements are the favorites of an audience interested in being well informed.

When your blog provides quality content and manages to do it frequently so as not to lose the public's interest, more and more users will take your opinions into account. This means that the public has developed trust towards your brand and has a positive image of it. Your brand enjoys a good reputation and gradually will become a voice of authority for your followers.

It is unnecessary to produce content that is too technical or border on academics if they do not go with the image you want to project for your brand. Remember that the most important thing is to save the quality: if, for example, you make a video, take care of the editing, the sound effects, the script, and the duration. Perhaps your product is aimed at a young audience who expects to see entertaining and straightforward videos or articles, but that does not mean you should offer imperfect or unfinished content.

On the other hand, the contents that have little work behind or only seek to generate sensationalism usually reflect a lower quality. The audience, which has become more intuitive and demanding, will realize the lack of work behind the content and stop taking it seriously. It is no surprise that low content deteriorates the brand's image and that most users pass by without reacting or commenting.

**Promote Your Brand**

Unlike traditional marketing, which is characterized by being annoying and invasive because it reaches the public when they least want it, inbound marketing seeks to get customers to come to you through the magic of content.

It is no longer about offering products or services directly to all your customers equally, as happened when listening to a radio spot or a television commercial that bursts in offering products that are not of interest to the majority. Content marketing is also not about those annoying banners that popped out of nowhere, invading your monitor, announcing that you had won an award for being visitor number 999.

The inbound marketing method consists of bringing information or entertainment to the public that interests, attracts, and falls in love with. People can choose what type of content they want to see and generally search for what is relevant.

This way of relating to customers and prospects has a positive effect on building the brand image. Users begin to identify those brands that offer them valuable information or simple moments of entertainment. If you manage to conquer them, they will be the ones who come to your blog or website because they will know that there they find the content they like.

All of this fulfills a vital function: promoting your brand and ensuring a positive impact on its image.

**Stand Out from The Competition**

One of the keys to branding is to distinguish your brand from your competitors. What makes your brand unique and different has to do with the value you offer to your customers, that is, the experience linked to your products or services. The value of a product has to do with the level of emotions, making the customer feel special:

receiving personalized treatment, a sense of belonging to a privileged group, following a fashion, etc.

Your content must be consistent with the value of your brand; how to achieve it? Creating unique content as stated earlier and having a seal of distinction for your brand. It can be a specific format, a typeface, a jingle, or address a particular weekly or monthly theme (for example, capsules on art, interviews with passersby). The possibilities are limitless.

Once you have a hallmark and have managed to capture the audience's attention, your brand image will have benefited, and luck will be on your side. When the public surfs the Internet and recognizes your content among everyone else, they will want to see yours without hesitation.

**Give Your Audience What They Ask For**

So far, you've heard the wonders of inbound marketing, but you may be wondering how to achieve that much-desired pull effect. The key is to segment your audience carefully before creating your content to know exactly who will read you. There is no point in creating content without first being clear to whom it is intended.

Therefore, studying the behavior of the public should be a core part of your content marketing strategy. This implies knowing their tastes, being aware of their trends and aspirations, and guiding the topics that you can develop. It is not the same to have an audience of young professionals than one of adolescent men or women over 60 years old.

Each buyer persona has different interests, comes from a particular socio-economic context, and has different concerns. Segment and get to know your buyer persona well so that you know what kind of information they expect to see while browsing the web: specialized information, tutorials, entertainment, news, curious facts, or tips.

Thanks to a detailed segmentation, you will also know what keywords they use in their searches and even what formats to use to offer the content: does your target audience prefer articles, memes, infographics, or videos? Do you like a serious, relaxed tone, or are you looking for some humor?

If you have enough dedication, you will come to distinguish a series of behavior patterns over time, and you can even predict how your audience will act in the future. So you will always know the right time to get the information so that there are more chances that your content will be seen and shared.

**Connects You with The Customer**

The contents can get closer to your clients and prospects, never like before, in a more subtle but more personalized way. Communication is bidirectional: not only does your brand communicate, but it is possible to interact with the public, listening to their comments, opinions, complaints, and suggestions, with the possibility of responding.

The contents shared through social media channels are an effective way to encourage users' participation with your brand. One way to do this is by inviting people to share experiences or photos related to the topic of your content, asking questions that the public is curious to answer, and adding the tags or hashtags of the moment.

To strengthen the public's connection, it is essential to include a call to action or call to action in your content: invite users to "like" your page or subscribe to your YouTube channel, include links to your website and buttons to share on social media platforms.

By following these strategies, the client develops trust towards the brand, generates engagement, and becomes their top of mind.

Content has a lot to offer to your brand's growth and plays a central role when building its identity. This is because they have become one of the main channels of contact with users.

Before offering your products and services directly, you must segment the public and study each buyer persona to offer engaging and exciting content. Having a strategy to regularly generate quality content is the best way to promote your brand and stand out from the competition.

# CHAPTER 9

## Using Social Media to Reinforce Brand Identity

Social networks are a vast virtual world to which people turn in search of entertainment and useful information, with communication, exchange of experience, discussion of current video content, posts, commercial products, and famous personalities. According to backlinko.com, in 2020, there are 3.81 billion people actively using social media in the world, and this is an increase of 9.2% year-on-year from 3.48 billion in 2019. Back in 2015, there were only 2.07 billion users; social network growth rates since then have averaged 12.5% year-on-year.

It is not surprising that entrepreneurs are looking for new channels of sales and dissemination of information about their products, services, and the brand began to consider this segment of Internet users as target customers of their selling sites. This is how the concept of SMM or social marketing (Social Media Marketing) was born, which today is an essential component of Internet marketing and implies a set of measures to promote a commercial product through social networks. Development of a competent SMM strategy, its step-by-step implementation in life, can attract a significant amount of new traffic to the target resource, increase sales, and make the brand recognizable and discussed.

In this chapter, we will analyze the main components of an SMM strategy and what results using this method can bring to those who keep up with the times and know that social networks are not mainly for likes and comments. But also a substantial potential channel for increasing efficiency for business identity; almost any business, and every user is a possible loyal customer.

Many people, especially newcomers to Internet commerce, imagine social marketing in a somewhat simplified way, as a simple choice of a particular social service and offering their product to the target audience. However, in reality, the social marketing strategy includes a considerable number of details, each of which must be considered. It is better to entrust the promotion in social networks to an SMM specialist who knows the field of Internet marketing, analyze audience requests, set precise tasks, and complete the plan actions for their implementation with a certain amount of creativity.

The strategy of SMM-promotion includes the following stages:

## 1. Highlighting The Company's Main Goals and Objectives Within the Framework of Its Presence in Social Networks.

This pivotal point answers key questions underlying social promotion: Why does a company need it, what are the expected results, and what means to use to get them.

## 2. Analysis of The Existing Brand Reputation in Social Networks, Comparison with Competitors.

It is worth keeping track of any mentions of the brand in communities, publics, groups, highlighting the most discussed commercial products, topics, and image points, determining the leading tone with which users of social networks speak about the company, and analyzing the reasons for the mentions.

Suppose the company is already present on social networks. In that case, the crucial moment is to assess the number of subscribers and their activity and analyze the page content (whether the information posted on it is useful and relevant).

The data obtained is compared with the ratings of competitors' social activity, based on which the steps must be taken to make your brand's position on social networks more advantageous compared to them. The task here is also to lure over a part of the audience of competitors, which can be achieved due to the posted content's quality and uniqueness and other points.

## 3. Defining The Target Audience and Drawing Up Its Portrait.

As previously identified in chapter 8 of this guide, Social network users unite into communities of different interests, ages, events. This must be taken into account when developing a different advertising strategy because advertising for a brand, a specific product, or service must meet subscribers' requests. This is the only way to attract a stream of users to the community's target site and company page. Otherwise, the advertising budget will be wasted.

For greater efficiency, it is desirable to divide the target audience into smaller segments. This tactic works well for narrowly targeted promotion (for example, advertising ovenware in communities on the topic of baking, advertising baby shoes for the smallest on pages where the main audience is young mothers, etc.).

## 4. Choosing A Social Platform for Presence.

It should be determined in which of the social networks there is the target group's maximum presence. You can use the results of third-party research and analyze competitive pages with similar topics and products. Having determined subscribers' activity to these pages, their number, interest in certain goods and services (reposts, likes, discussions), it is easy to understand how this audience matches the products you are promoting in terms of their requests.

## 5. Creation of A Platform for Communication of the Target Audience.

It is not so much the vital format here, but how attractive the platform will be to new visitors. To do this, it must be "live", that is, it must be continuously filled with new information materials relevant to target subscribers and be open for comments.

## 6. Development of A Plan for Writing and Posting Content.

This strategically important point has been discussed in more detail in the last chapter. It is the content that shapes users' attitude towards your company, helps to gain trust and attract more subscribers, and therefore potential customers, in the long term.

Content strategy is something that you should never save on. Investments in the content do not pay off immediately: it will take up to six months for the costs to begin to bear fruit, but after all, audience loyalty cannot be won in a short period. It is necessary to determine the concept of filling the platform: what the company wants to announce to its subscribers, how it will do it, how often new posts are supposed to be posted, highlight the main categories of content.

In terms of promotion, the so-called viral content works great, which usually has an entertainment format. It is he who is most often liked; subscribers share and actively comment.

In addition to the entertainment function, information can also have other purposes:

**Educational:**

Educational posts work for the company's image, help to gain the reputation of a serious brand and, at the same time, provide valuable information to the audience, help find solutions in certain situations, and provide answers to targeted user requests.

**Commercial:**

These types of publications include selling advertising posts that help promote a particular product or service. The percentage of such posts should not be large to irritate the audience: you need to intersperse them with materials of a different nature. Otherwise, instead of clicking on the links, you will receive a sea of negative reviews and un-subscriptions from your page.

**Informational (news, product reviews, stories about the internal life of the company, etc.)**

It is desirable to make news posts unique to interest subscribers. News can be general and publications about corporate life events, such as exhibitions, achievements, holidays, and stories about innovations in the production process. Do not hesitate to post as many photos and videos as possible: visual information catches the eye and interests, evokes a feeling of sincerity in your attitude towards the audience. The more open a brand positions itself, the easier it is to gain the trust of subscribers.

It is worth highlighting user-generated content in a particular category, that is, posts from your customers that tell about your company and its products (reviews of products with photo and video materials, recommendations for use).

**7. High-Quality Graphic Design of the Group.**

The page's appearance should work for brand recognition and reputation, so you shouldn't save money here either. A branded cover, various postcards for the holidays with a company logo, design designs for presentations, announcements of contests and sweepstakes, a single template for posts, and periodic changes to the design are necessary components of an SMM marketing strategy.

**8. Definition of Channels for an Advertising Campaign.**

It is necessary to attract subscribers and customers to the created platform and the selling site, and this flow must be constant.

For these purposes, various promotion methods are used:

Advertising in social networks, aimed at the target audience.

Targeting: You can make ads visible only to a limited number of users who fall into the criteria you specified for gender, age, location, position, events, interests, etc.

Advertising in popular communities with many subscribers, good traffic, and activity (guest posts).

For example, contest and prize draw among those subscribers who repost, a review of a product/service, a photo with a company's product. Also, contests can be creative if you need to compose a poem, come up with a slogan, make a creative photo or drawing to participate in the drawing.

Promotion by working with famous bloggers, "Instagrammers," and other people whose opinions strongly influence the audience, shaping its requests.

## 9. Tracking Conversion Efficiency Indicators

Implementation of the SMM promotion strategy in practice can take place with different efficiency. To determine which posts, advertising campaigns attract the audience and bring the result expected according to the strategy's goals, and which promotion methods should be abandoned due to their un-profitableness, it is customary to highlight the main parameters for tracking performance or Know Performance Indicators (KPIs).

These include items such as the number of subscribers in the group, audience coverage by a specific publication, subscriber activity concerning the post, the number of reposts, positive reviews in relation to their total number, the number of posted user content, the number of visits to the site, the conversion of site visitors (i.e., how many transitions turned into real orders), financial costs for each transition.

When the SMM promotion process has already been launched, there is no need to be afraid to make adjustments. Analytics are needed to highlight the most effective actions, to use and redistribute the advertising budget, costs for specialists (designer, copywriter, etc.), time, and human resources.

Simultaneously, unique content, creativity, and open communication with subscribers attract the audience, helping to reduce advertising costs. Fill the group with new materials regularly, comment on reviews, create communities in several social networks, entrust their management to those who have sufficient knowledge for this. Your platform will become an essential part of the business, will contribute to creating a positive brand identity, become integral, and maybe, and the primary source of profit.

# CHAPTER 10

## Brand Extension

Expansion of the brand range (brand extension) is the use of the company's existing brand to enter new markets or segments, increase the range of the company by releasing new products under the existing brand of the company.

### *10.1 The Strategies*

Two main strategies for expanding the range

There are 2 types of brand assortment extension: linear and categorical extension.

#### Linear Extension

A line extension uses an existing brand name to release new varieties of products within an existing market or product category. For example: expanding the existing assortment of biscuits by releasing a new flavor or large packaging; expansion of the existing range of vehicles by launching a new sports model.

#### Categorical Extension

Category extension is using the name of an existing brand to enter an entirely new market. For example, using an existing brand of cookies to enter a new milk market (which is healthier to eat cookies with), or using an existing car brand to enter a new motorcycle market.

## Extension Efficiency

Suppose your company has decided to expand its product or service range. In that case, there are three things to consider: the size of the cannibalization of the range, the alignment of the new product with the brand image, and the company's ability to market the new product.

## Cannibalization of Assortment

Almost any new product takes over part of the existing assortment sales. Therefore, when expanding the company's assortment, a transparent economic model should be calculated, which will include the following indicators:

- New product sales and profit
- Cannibalization (replacement of sales) with new products of the old assortment
- Sales volume and profit of the old assortment without the release of a new one
- Sales volume and profit of the new assortment taking into account the release of the new product

If, as a result of the model, the sales and profits for the entire assortment without the release of a novelty are comparable to or less than the sales and profits of the assortment with the release of a novelty, then such an expansion is meaningless. The cannibalization percentage is calculated expertly based on the experience of existing extensions of the product line.

## Compliance of The Product with The Brand Image

The new product mustn't undermine the brand identity or contradict its approved positioning. If new products have lower consumer qualities, they can reduce the overall brand impression of the company. Therefore, you should strictly monitor that they are no worse than existing products and fit into the product's target audience's idea.

**Distribution Opportunities**

Before launching a new product, it is necessary to generally look at the distribution of the company's existing assortment in the market. Suppose a company cannot provide an acceptable distribution of the current assortment. In that case, all efforts should focus on the growth of distribution indicators for current products and not load the dealer channel with new products.

For example, suppose out of all your assortment in most retail outlets, there are only 5 out of 10 positions. In that case, the release of an additional 11 position will only lead to replacing one of the existing ones on the shelf. This will lead to almost 100% cannibalization and is ineffective from a business point of view.

## 10.2 The Pressure to Grow

Also, in today's environment, the pressure on companies to grow, achieve more market share, and greater profitability leading companies to search for new uses, markets, channels, and consumers has turned the extensions of Brand into one of the priorities of the annual marketing and branding agendas and plans.

According to a Nielsen study of brands conducted in the US and UK, brand extensions are five times more successful than new launches: leveraging the reputation, quality, credibility, and authority previously established by the parent brand significantly increase the chances of success. The ease and cost savings that can be made when launching new products or developments is a temptation for any company and is a factor that encourages venturing.

However, the risks can be irreversible and must be carefully assessed since the damage inflicted on the 'mother brand' is not irrelevant (image, contraindications...). There are sounded successes and sounded failures in the field of product branding.

But what happens in the market? Until when, where, and how can a brand be extended? As we've understood from the beginning of this chapter, a brand extension is a branding and marketing strategy that uses an existing brand (an umbrella brand) and developed to launch another product under the same name, but another category of products.

An example is Colgate, a well-known toothpaste that years ago also extended to toothbrushes. In Spain, the case of Don Simon draws our attention: juices, chicken broths, wines, horchata, vegetable milk... all under the same brand. It was the original tetra brick of wines that did much to link and transfer the price/quality ratio of the product. So far, they got! Another example would be Kit-Kat (from chocolate bars to ice cream, etc.)

Unlike a brand extension, the product extension could be considered an extension for a new variety in the same product category. A technique often used for flavors uses, or even formats, such as Ariel Pods versus Basic or Actilift.

Also, Coke launched its variety of light or zero across the range of queues, and Fairy dishwasher by hand extended its products to the dishwasher by machine.

In addition to fragrances, glasses, and cosmetics, Armani has launched a chain of hotels, a lifestyle and experience similar to those that the fashion brand itself can offer.

**Advantages of Brand Extensions**

As we said, brand extensions are a temptation for any brand manager due to their extensive benefits and the business opportunities they represent. Its favorable points also include:

- They allow the brand's access and reach to new uses and audiences, increasing its base, accessibility, visibility, resonance, and presence.
- They allow extending the credibility and authority of the brand image to new prospects and markets.
- Brand capital improvement
- They improve the emotional connection of the brand with its audiences.
- They extend and optimize meanings for the brand, which opens towards broader, meaningful, and relevant positions and purposes.
- They reduce the risk of choosing a new product/brand.
- They reinforce the associations they share with the parent brand.
- They allow building for other new extensions in the future.

**Risks of Brand Extensions**

On the other hand, the risks that they can represent if they are not done correctly are:

- Reputational risk: disappointment or non-fulfillment of expectations (quality, results that do not comply, failures ...)
- Irrelevance of the offered proposal, which does not mean or does not interest new users. There could be an emotional disconnect from the parent brand in some interest segments unhappy with the extension.
- Inappropriateness, lack of credibility, contradiction, or incompatibility with the extension's values or associations

with the mother brand. The non-existence of transferable elements

- Irrelevance of the new category of the transferred: the values of the parent brand may be irrelevant in or for the new category
- Perceptual cannibalization with the mother brand. And also in sales, especially if it is a product extension.
- Confusion: loss of focus of the parent brand itself, which is diluted, ambiguous, or blurred and not associated with any specific category. It can also happen due to an excess of extensions that make it lose its center of gravity or identity.
- Creation of new and unwanted associations or perceptions for the mother brand derived from the extension itself.

A real example of these dangers was experienced by a traditional company when Colgate launched a precooked lasagna in the United States because the food would later cause the need for oral hygiene.

In short, and although an extension is an always tempting temptation, it is necessary to correctly analyze and evaluate all these risks and avoid acting lightly. In extensions, think twice: where, how, and why.

## 10.3 Product Line and Brand Family Expansion Strategy

As noted, as part of a brand strategy, companies can focus on multiple brands operating in the same market, extend a brand name to a range of products, or assign a different name to each product.

With the expansion of the product line, new products appear in the existing product category under the existing brand name. For example, creating products of new shapes, sizes, designs, changing packaging.

Another option is the multiband strategy, where the company develops its name for each product. Accordingly, a multi-brand is a trademark from one product category, but with its personality. A classic example: Procter & Gamble, which makes detergents under the brand names Tide, Bold, Dash, Cheer, and Oxydol.

When the differences between markets are large, companies practice collecting products under one umbrella, expanding the brand family, using a strong brand to promote products to other market segments. For example, the successful Yamaha brand, which has established itself in the motorcycle market, produces musical instruments and sports equipment.

The expansion of the brand family can be done horizontally or vertically. Horizontal expansion is aimed primarily at differentiating distribution channels by providing distributors and retailers with specific brands. Many companies do this when they designate their products for sale in low-cost stores and specialty stores. Thus, the manufacturer helps to increase its market share and improves its distribution network.

The vertical expansion involves applying a consumer differentiation strategy when a brand is created for a specific group of consumers with specific needs. The most effective way to conquer new market segments is to create a new brand with its image, sales, and service system. The vertical multi-brand system is focused on high profits, and at the same time, the main problem of this strategy is the high cost of forming a brand identity. For example, Toyota had to invest heavily in marketing, distribution, and service to move its Lexus brand into a new automotive market segment.

In a modern market, the role of strategies for expanding product lines and brands and assigning them the names of well-known manufacturing companies is increasing. This is primarily due to the high market rejection of new products and significant long-term investments in measures to promote consumer acceptance of the brand. It is cheaper to launch a new product based on a well-known brand.

All of the concept studies show that new brand-name products generate a lot of customer interest and a willingness to make a trial purchase. This is because a successful trade name, in this case, acts as an indirect quality guarantee for new products released under this name.

The choice of a brand expansion option or an individual approach to the name depends on the brand positioning strategy.

- If products are intended for the same market segment, they can successfully appear under the same trademark or be called a company name.
- If the same products are intended for different target audiences, it is advisable to use the company name for them. Companies often use an additional degree of identification for brand positioning to highlight its prestige or exceptional quality in such a situation.
- If the manufacturer offers products within the same segment of the target market, but with different distinctive advantages

## 10.4 The Brand Generation

The relationship between brand policies and the historical moment of a company during a generational change. In most cases, companies are not considered when instead. It would be an opportunity to intervene on the brand identity and could be useful to make the disclosure of the new vision more effective.

Statistically, the generational shift is marked by significant corporate reorganization changes, often generating problems of acceptance of the new course or friction on the way to its implementation.

The new generation needs to convince their stakeholders, both internally and towards the market, that their vision is necessary and not a whim of the incoming management. In this context, a renewed brand identity would have the power to create immediate engagement on users, making the reasons for the change understandable.

And a more coherent brand-strategy to the company's new paradigms would give greater resonance to a historical event such as the generational change. The whole organization must recognize itself, and people can transform themselves into active and not passive witnesses within the evolutionary process.

The most discriminating factors of change, during a generational change, in rethinking the corporate identity, can be equally endogenous and exogenous: the evolution of the supply system or the market's renewed needs. Other causes can be linked to a greater push towards foreign countries, both in territorial expansion and markets. Acting on the brand and the institutional identity is increasingly a critical success factor to make these changes credible.

The new generation of a company must take office without risking losing the value that the brand itself has acquired thanks to previous generations' work. To do it correctly and know how to analyze and rationalize everything from the past that will have to be "ferried" and therefore valorized within the new generational course, a delicate component lies in the management of the company staff, from staff to Commercial network. Before defining the new corporate identity and presenting it externally, it will be necessary to involve the internal public in a preventive manner.

Often we find ourselves facing the development of brand identity in a situation characterized by the passage between generations and, sometimes, also having to consider the coexistence between the new one and the previous one. For example, in the latter case, the change in governance is more complex, especially in family businesses, because it is necessary to analyze the present and plan the future considering the past in a much more articulated way.

Then there are situations in which the new generation almost wants to cancel the previous one: the most relevant aspects mainly concern the timing. Ownership or management has a clear understanding of the new vision, but it takes time to make it tangible and operational.

# CHAPTER 11

## Developing an Authentic Brand Story That Improves Trust

**B**eing excellent is no longer enough in today's environment; you need authentic and compelling stories we identify and remember.

### 11.1 Does Your Brand Have a Powerful Story?

Undoubtedly one of the best, most effective, and efficient ways to obtain a competitive advantage in today's environment, where brands tend to be undifferentiated and mean nothing. To distinguish ourselves from the herd, let's tell an authentic story that identifies us and makes us unique.

The stories are what connect us, but because they spend hours connected to social networks. People long for powerful emotional connections that only stories can make, which leads us to the vital empathy for any business's success in today's reality. As soon as we think about it, the brands we connect with, be it a "monster" like Nike or a small brand, have compelling, compelling, and in many cases, provocative stories that make their audiences feel motivated and connected.

The most memorable stories of the brand, try to connect unexpectedly, speak directly, are emotional, and try to go to the heart; the best way for rationality to nullify a connection or sale. Although overused, let's take Nike as an example. The brand's stories revolve around "Just Do It," challenging people to adopt a spirit of improvement, even sometimes rebellious, that consistently and truly authentically impacts consumers around the world emotionally, which leads it to be a leader in categories as different as Golf or athletics.

Let's get down to business; why is it so important to tell stories around a business?

An authentic brand story makes you memorable.

It differentiates you and generates positive and human connections.

Bring the brand to life.

Define and understandably the competitive advantage it brings.

It contributes to the segmentation of the brand's target market, in some cases allowing diversification.

It positions you at a strategic level.

## Does Your Brand Have a Powerful Story?

Once we have understood this, the next step is to incorporate stories as brand creation and management tools. What requires taking on a new role in brand management, as captain of a ship that leads the brand through stormy seas, now it's time to add another element to the dashboard to keep the right course. You need to be very aware of the brand's attitude, personality, and tone to start developing stories that convey subliminal messages that take on a life of their own, ideally from the consumer side.

The tremendous success is that the story transcends the brand and becomes the patrimony of its consumers. Coca Cola, Harley Davidson, Jack Daniels, or Zara do not need to tell their story since they have those who do it for them in a much more effective and authentic way.

An essential element is that the story is credible, authentic, and where possible positive and inspiring. If your story does not come close to this, it is best to go back to your inspiration space and start over. Most of the brands that succeed are characterized by high levels of "energy" that they transmit through their stories, even from their leaders. Thus, brands like Apple, Virgin, Nike, Facebook, and many more are brands with high energy and great personality, which transmit magnetic power. Now that you know that your brand needs to transmit vitality, energy, and strength, it is time to redirect your stories' creation.

People have the "strange" ability to detect brands with personality and energy and fall in love with them. Therefore, it seems that a brand with personality is more likely to succeed, so let's get away from "bland" communications, the monotonous and boring tone and start working on an attractive personality, which in many cases happens to be a brand that is a little "eccentric", energetic and passionate that he infects his energy.

This is an element that the CEO–if this is not the representation of the brand and the rest of the brand members must always consider when transmitting strength and passion for the business, which is always it goes through a high consistency and alignment of the messages.

Just like a car works best when the wheels are aligned or a football team when in sync, brand communication to be effective must be consistent and coherent. Thus, beyond the alignment in the different on and off channels and the synergies that are generated, the entire organization, from the way of answering the phone to how the customer is welcomed- must work to reinforce the personality and brand energy, which in the end is a manifestation of the brand's stories. In short, for the brand to connect with its audiences, it must be authentic and passionate and manifest it consistently. Being direct

100

and clear is an excellent start to start shaping brand stories that connect, defining exactly who we are in compelling and credible ways. This ultimately translates into the personal values and beliefs that identify us and what inspires and motivates us, which must revolve around their stories that will give life to the brand.

## 11.2 Tell a Story

Today we're going to tell you a story! That of storytelling. Very fashionable lately, storytelling is today one of the most effective levers to build and heal its reputation. But how could storytelling help achieve this goal? Close-up on this practice, already widely acclaimed by notable brands!

You might have understood it by reading the introduction of this chapter: storytelling is the art of telling stories. Be careful; this is not about reading a lullaby to your prospects. Storytelling is merely getting your key messages across in a story that will captivate your targets.

Besides, storytelling has become highly prized, especially across the Atlantic. American brands (Nike, Walt Disney, Apple, etc.) have been using storytelling for a long time and have seen that it helps build customer loyalty. Touched by the history of a company, it will indeed be more attached to it. And it's quite natural! But if you look more at the literal meaning of this phrase, you will agree that the art of storytelling is a long-standing practice.

In an environment where consumers are less and less sensitive to advertising, it is difficult to capture their attention on a product or service. For them, traditional marketing campaigns have indeed become too intrusive, even aggressive. Most of them no longer take the time to view an advertising message, read a marketing email, or even less listen to a salesperson give them a long argument. Consumers, especially Millennials, value authenticity.

**Keep It Real**

To get them interested again, you have to think about taking a different approach. By opting for storytelling, you humanize your speech to convey your message to your target audience more quickly. Indeed, it is easier to grab your audience's attention with a great story rather than a long list of facts and arguments. By playing the emotional card, you make them more receptive and, at the same time, win their support for your brand. It is precisely the same spring as we regularly write to you about the experience.

In short, between a brand that holds a very impersonal discourse, and another that plays the card of proximity, prospects will naturally be attracted by the second!

## 11.3 Successful Storytelling: Some Tips and Tricks

Mastering storytelling requires several qualities. The first imposes know-how in the art of staging. You have to set the scene, including specifying the place, presenting and describing the characters, and highlighting the context. The goal is to create images in your audience's minds, just like in any narrative work. It is also essential that you have great creativity. Your story must arouse emotion with your target, capture their intention, and convince them to join your brand.

In practice, storytelling requires a perfect knowledge of your target. To know what kind of story this one might be sensitive to, you need to look at its specifics. In B2B, it is about answering various questions: what type of clientele are you targeting (companies, employees, media, etc.)? What is your target audience (industry, number of employees, turnover, etc.)? What is he looking for? Where is he? Once you have gathered all the data on your target, it will be easier to determine which language to use to reach it. Note, however, that storytelling is intended to be fun and complicit, so avoid being too formal.

## Marketing Storytelling

It is also essential that the story you tell, whether fictional or real, is in perfect harmony with your identity. This sincerity will be perceived by the public, who will then hasten to follow you to know the rest of your story or learn more about your brand.

Okay, but what does it have to do with marketing?

Remember: the main objective is not to sell a product or a service. It is instead to make sure that your brand gains the attention and the affection of the public. Developing an inbound marketing strategy will allow you to convert your audience but, above all, make your customers the main ambassadors of your brand. But how do you retain visitors to your website?

For example, you can request your visitors' email address in exchange for a free e-book or training offered: you will thus develop your mailing list, and you will be able to create a unique link with your audience. Add call-to-action buttons, create exciting landing pages: all these elements will allow you to attract your audience to a captivating sales funnel.

Eventually, to monitor your strategy's success, it is essential to define precise indicators, as stated in previous chapters of this guide. For example, it could be the engagement on your social networks, your number of subscribers to your newsletter, or the bounce rate of your site.

As you can see, to stand out online and make your brand unforgettable, you must integrate your storytelling strategy into your overall strategy. Storytelling will allow you to enhance your content marketing strategy and be a powerful lever in your inbound marketing strategy.

# CHAPTER 12

## Branding and Packaging

There are many different packaging types, the most popular of which are indeed the slip-on lids, hinged boxes, or sliding boxes. Which packaging is the right one for which purpose is often not an easy decision?

**Individual Packaging for All Purposes: Choose The Type of Packaging.**

Roughly speaking, it can be said: the sliding box and the slip-lid box are suitable for small to medium-sized packaging. Too large formats should be avoided with these two variants. With increasing size, the individual elements (insert or cover) become less easy to use and more difficult to open.

On the other hand, the hinged packaging is wonderfully suitable for the production of medium to large formats. Overall, thanks to the simple opening mechanism, it is easy to use in large formats and has a robust stature.

## *12.1 Considerations Based On Optical Aspects.*

Of course, not only the handling but also the look of the packaging plays a significant role. Different types of packaging also have different functions that can be used. Think, for example, of the inner part of the lid of a hinged packaging. This can be used, for example, to attach a storage compartment to accommodate all kinds of content.

The slip lid or the slide-in box can be differentiated from one another, for example, in terms of color or material. Think, for example, of the combination of different materials. A very smooth structure in the lower part and a raised structure on the lid can create exciting haptic contrasts.

**Economic Aspects**

Of course, economic considerations should also not be ignored. Hinged boxes are a little more complex to manufacture, and therefore a little higher in price than telescopic or sliding boxes. This is due to the respective material use within the production of the respective type of packaging.

**What Else Should You Know?**

There are minimum dimensions for the production of high-quality cardboard boxes. It can be said that slip-lid boxes can be manufactured from a width of approx. 70 mm. With sliding boxes or hinged boxes, however, you should calculate at least 100mm in width. A minimum height of approx. 20 mm can only rarely be avoided. Fine cardboard boxes can be made in all conceivable material thicknesses. In principle, it is advisable to set the base material thickness to at least 2mm for large formats;

## 12.2 What Criteria Do Customers Use to Rate Packaging?

The packaging is considered the hub between the customer and the product, especially at the point of sale and product presentation in B2B business relationships. The packaging determines how a product is perceived and influences the respective viewer in their purchase decision. The packaging combines different functions: On the one hand, it is a marketing tool, is needed for product protection, and often has to act as an information carrier. Last but not least, the packaging should, of course, also increase the quality of the product and attract attention.

The packaging should be the right size, be as economical as possible to produce and match the product's shape and color and the brand. When it comes to the conception of a successful packaging solution, the product must be targeted on the one hand and the brand (in particular the respective corporate design) or the company on the other. But customers, any competition or legal requirements must also be observed.

**Reusability, Design, and Environmental Friendliness Are Very Important.**

While the production process and the packaging design are mostly in the hands of the respective company, it is more difficult to find out what is convincing for the customer in terms of packaging.

Reusable packaging, for example, is viral. There is a little to sort out because consumers have different demands depending on the product. As a rule, a gummy bear bag is not expected to be reusable, but the situation is different from the packaging of a high-quality accessory or technical device. Buyers expect matching packaging when purchasing a high-priced product, so the requirement for reusability is automatically given here.

**The Perfect Design Convinces at The Decisive Moment.**

In the purchase phase or at the moment of presentation, for example, at a trade fair or in a meeting, the packaging design decides whether it is so-called sales packaging or presentation packaging because the first point of contact with a product is the packaging, which at the same time has the task of conveying the value of the content, underlining it and captivating the viewer.

An all-solving formula for success is impossible in packaging design, packaging that attracts attention, looks authentic and appears tangible. Simultaneously, it conveys the essentials but has an excellent basis to become an eye-catcher. It is essential to create a recognition value for the company using the packaging design, i.e., customers who have already held packaging, for example, another product of the same brand, should directly link it when they pick up the new packaging. So, of course, also to the manufacturer or a brand. This can be achieved, for example, through a particularly striking, in some cases simple, the precise interplay of color and geometry, but also through tactile elements such as embossing, lacquering, or engraving. The viewer remembers optical features and tangible experiences and evaluates packaging in the interplay of several sensory organs.

## *How Important Is the Idea of Sustainability to Consumers and Companies?*

Environmentally-friendly business and consumption are part of buyers' and sellers' philosophy in almost all areas, including packaging. Regardless of whether it is about tea packaging or adequate cardboard packaging for high-quality material samples. Recycling and the entire life cycle are at the center of the assessment, and packaging with so-called secondary uses is closely linked.

An essential factor in the sustainable use of our resources and our environment is the durability of products, which also includes packaging. Reusable boxes fulfill new functions after their actual use and may replace new purchases. It can be safely summarized that when it comes to packaging, an appealing visual design, creativity, stability, and ecological aspects are very important. Overall, however, there are no general statements to be made. The demands of many consumers and companies vary depending on the product segment.

## 12.3 Do It Yourself Packaging Design: Helpful Tips

Packaging has not only had protective functions for a long time. Packaging should also embody the content, speak representative of a brand, or a product. Creative and functional packaging design generates attention, communicates, and evokes particular emotions in the customer. Most importantly, it sells.

**Packaging Design: An Art in Itself.**

**1. Keep It Simple**

Sometimes less is more. The largest and most successful corporations worldwide now rely on straightforward typography, a minimalist logo, and an overall clear packaging design. Overloaded packaging is clearly on a downward trend (if you leave out the food industry). Clear packaging always appears to be of high quality, representative and is often given new tasks, for example, as a case, casket, or other storage boxes.

**2. Create Unpacking Experiences**

It is hard to believe, but whole teams work to give the end-user an extraordinary feeling when unpacking. Various packaging concepts are opened and closed again here for months. Because the so-called box opening has become an essential part of packaging design. A wide variety of techniques and functions are available here, such as banderoles, fine tissue paper, or unusual closure techniques.

**3. Try Something Different**

Products that are usually packaged in a certain way can also be wrapped outside of the norm. This allows you to stand out from the crowd and leave an unmistakable impression. Consumers appreciate creativity and are also willing to put a higher price on the table for the product as a whole.

## 4. Let The Packaging for The Product Communicate

If a product has unique properties, these should be conveyed through the packaging design. Ingenuity and creativity are required here. Does the product come from the manufacture, i.e., handcraft? Then, for example, packaging in the so-called handcrafted look would be a suitable concept.

## 5. Humor Always Attracts

Packaging designs that put a smile on the viewer's face always have a sales-promoting effect. Such an effect can be achieved on the one hand through unusual packaging functions, on the other hand, also through humorous sayings or typography.

## 6. Show Your Colors

Black, gray, or white packaging is beautiful and straightforward, but bright colors can also be used wonderfully in the packaging design. Provided it fits the brand and the product. Especially in spring and summer, the packaging looks so fresh and simple fitting.

## 7. Stay Straight

If products are intended for shipping, additional shipping packaging is usually required. Sales packaging regularly does not survive the post. Here, too, care should be taken to design the appropriate shipping boxes to receive the impression of something extraordinary when they receive the goods before coming into contact with the final packaging.

## Packaging Impacting Brand Identity and Sales

All information about a product must reach the consumer by sight. Hence the importance of standing out through unique packaging. The proper packaging of packaging is an attractive path to success to promote a product or its brand.

### a. Preserve The Customer Relationship

The choice of packaging can have real impacts on its sales, on the brand's image, or even the location in-store that's the brand's identity at large. The right packaging stimulates customer relations. A long-term relationship requires quality conditioning without limits. As part of the first approach to consumption or prospecting, the packaging is already an invaluable means of communication and promotion of the item for sale.

### b. Influence On Consumers' Decision

A well-crafted blanket should convey an apprehensible and understandable message. The flagship product is highlighted and must be able to influence the decision of buyers fully. The more aesthetically pleasing the package, the better! Therefore, we must try to seduce the consumer from the printing of labels, the choice of colors, to typography. Therefore, the aim is to increase as much as possible; the attention paid visually to the product. Especially since the chance of consumption increases.

### c. Personalized Packaging Printing: To Make Yourself Distinct

Intending to promote a consumer excellent and duplicate sales, personalized packaging printing is fundamental. To make a different commercial identity manifest and stand out significantly from the competition, personalization is essential. If 35.5% of self-service buyers bet on the package, both useful and aesthetic, it is wise to opt for the most innovative and original possible. Consumers will be able to spot the good from afar. In terms of packaging, specificities matter as much as design; the incentive to purchase is forged through profit-sharing. A powerful, authentic, and clear message is therefore required.

### d. Make Manifest Your Pro-Ecological Position

According to the Environment Law, all products must be packaged according to the provisions stipulated therein. In this way, many companies are deploying sustainable personalized packaging manufacturing and printing solution. They present the considerable impact of their product and packaging on the environment. With regard to ecology, packages of recyclable materials and natural origins are preferred. However, packaging can prove to be a considerable pro-ecological positioning means. This displays an authentic image of the brand.

### e. Interactive Packaging

In terms of personalized packaging printing, the company or brand can provide additional information to connect directly with consumers or even establish an interaction. With the arrival of this type of packaging, we can say that adhesive advertising is no longer relevant. Packaging can be interactive as long as it presents QR codes. The use of codes involves scanning per minute via a smartphone or tablet, which will allow the brand to promote its entire range of products. The creation of a customer database followed as well as the establishment of a prestigious brand identity.

# CHAPTER 13

## Branding and Advertising

The process of forming and promoting brands (branding) is often associated exclusively with advertising. When it comes to a marketing program, many managers' first idea is the thought of advertising: where to place it and how much money should be allocated for it. The decision to launch a new brand is made depending on the cost of the advertising campaign.

Such an approach is not only fundamentally wrong: its implementation most often leads to excessive and unproductive waste of funds. The eminent advertising specialist E. Rice believes that this deep and dangerous misconception leads to the fact that most companies spend too much on advertising at the stage of brand creation when money needs to be invested in PR, and too little when the brand has already taken shape and needs advertising support.

The point is that it is impossible to create a brand through advertising. Other methods, mainly PR, solve this task. Advertising can only provide and support an already created brand, remind about it. Who will pay attention to advertising for a new unknown brand? Why on earth would anyone believe these calls? Aggressive advertising elicits natural psychological resistance. The consumer treats her with a certain degree of skepticism and irony, at least does not feel unconditional trust in her loud statements. Surveys worldwide show that advertising is one of the least trusted occupations, behind, for example, nurses by a factor of eight.

Advertising is the seller's voice; therefore, from the point of view of the consumer, it is initially biased. All of them shout, "Buy it from me!" While the buyer has no opportunity to verify the authenticity of what the purchased artists and purchased designers are trying to convince him of. Advertising can even be alarming.

Trust in advertising arises only on the foundation of fame, recommendation; until the new brand gets it, active advertising will be counterproductive.

Figuratively speaking, advertising cannot kindle a fire, but it can prevent the flame from going out.

The advertising campaign should follow PR both in terms of timing and subject matter. It should be started only after PR's goals have been achieved, and its subject matter should correspond to the images and ideas formed among potential consumers by means of PR. An expensive advertising campaign should only be started for an up-and-coming brand.

The main thing in modern business is not advertising and not even a product, but the image of a product. The question is how to ensure that a potential buyer has a favorable image of the product and its manufacturer. Advertising has not seen any noticeable success in addressing this issue. It cannot change consumers' views and replace a brand that already exists in their minds with a new one. Advertising can successfully interact only with the ideas that have developed in people's minds and develop them no more, but no less. Coca-Cola is not drunk because something is happening to polar bears in its ads.

Effective branding presupposes creating a new niche in the market, i.e., in the minds of a potential consumer, and the opportunity to become the first in it. In doing so, you need to ensure sufficient incentive to move customers from the old to the new. It is easy to say but very difficult to do. All respectable marketing science warns against doing this. The first question a marketer usually asks is, "What is the size of the market?" However, for a new brand, for a new niche, the market size is zero.

If you manage to create a new niche, become the first in it and find a powerful incentive for consumers, you can be sure that the advertising "get-together" will immediately offer you help.

All major successes and breakthroughs in the market of recent times have been achieved with PR's help and not advertising. Some of the most prominent and well-known examples are Wal-Mart, Microsoft, Yahoo!, Amazon.com, Body shop, Harry Potter, PlayStation, Oracle. Wal-Mart has become the world's largest retailer, with little to no advertising spend.

The main difference between PR and advertising is the use of information sources independent of the manufacturer. As the volume and aggressiveness of advertising grow, people become suspicious and wary. They seek advice and information from independent, authoritative sources. People are more likely to trust the information that they receive not during advertising time or on advertising media space, but in news materials, the opinion of experts, celebrities, their friends, and finally themselves. For a modern person, all these are islands of objectivity in a sea of bias and biasedness.

When faced with advertising, a person thinks: "If what these guys are talking about were true, I would definitely know about it." Therefore, for advertising to be effective, it needs preliminary confirmation to know about it from independent sources, preferably authoritative for them.

## 13.1 Opinions and Experiences I

On checking one of the popular dailies, I saw a "basement" on a third of the page that Israeli doctors have discovered a drug against cancer.

The article is written in detail, with a detailed description of the discovery itself and the drug's action. At the end of the material, it is said that the USA, along with Russia, Germany, and Japan, is included in the first wave of drug distribution since most of the specialists who made this discovery are from the USSR.

Therefore, the reader can send a napkin with two drops of blood to the indicated address, and the drug will be selected for him. The first reaction that occurred already during the reading: Why haven't I heard of this discovery before? Why wasn't such a landmark breakthrough reported in the news? Why did none of the famous people report this? Why didn't I read about it in glossy weeklies in news blocks or science news? Only towards the end of the reading, you notice that the material is framed.

Advertising! A sick person will send a napkin, cling to every chance, every opportunity. But you understand that this is just an advertisement; it would inspire confidence if I had already heard about this discovery and preparation: from the news, from the opinions of authoritative and famous people, from friends, and this is PR.

In the information society, victory or defeat is determined by public consciousness, in the formation of which the media (including the Internet) play a crucial role. If the battle for public acceptance is lost in the media, it is also lost in the marketplace.

To start promoting a brand, sometimes one favorable phrase in an article or TV show, a mention in the speech of a famous politician or a movie or pop star is enough. They can be used an infinite number of times in various publications and broadcasts, citing and placing in the most prominent place.

## 13.2 Opinions and Experiences II

116

The Polaroid brand was created in a matter of hours: as soon as Polaroid showed off the instant photograph, Dr. Land and his new camera hit the cover of The Time magazine, and the information about them was on the news programs of national TV channels and virtually all local media.

The Xerox brand also emerged almost immediately after demonstrating the new copier and subsequent publications discussing the novelty.

It is essential to demonstrate your uniqueness immediately. Thus, advertising increases sales, and PR fosters brand loyalty. This means that the task of PR is to maintain positive brand identity, but advertisers also see their goal in creating a brand identity and image.

The role of advertising in creating and maintaining a company's image is enormous. Low-quality advertising quite naturally evokes negative emotions from the public, which are transferred to the firm itself. This must not be forgotten. Also, the process of creating an effective advertising campaign is very delicate and time-consuming. Each professionally executed ad is not a single shot but a long-term contribution to the firm's brand identity. It links a series of messages addressed to the same consumers, a fragment of an ongoing, consistent campaign.

Nevertheless, for all the closeness of advertising and PR, there are two relatively straightforward criteria for their difference. Firstly, advertising is associated with the positioning of a product in the market. PR is with the positioning not so much of a product as of a company (including its top officials) and not so much in the market as in society as a whole. Secondly, advertising costs are usually included in the production costs of a particular product and, thus, they are directly included in its price. The costs of PR, as a rule, are covered from the budget (fund) for the development of the company (abroad - the strategic budget). When calculating prices, they are taken into account indirectly.

A superficial and frivolous attitude to the specifics and differences between advertising and PR often leads to severe mistakes.

Advertising is an operating cost and will not pay off in the future as it protects the brand in the present. As a reminder, advertising can and should be witty, engaging, intriguing, funny, dramatic, well-conceived, played, and orchestrated: it should have all the properties of good advertising except creativity. Advertising should not be new and original: a product, product, or service should be unique.

Like the common cold, a brand is best communicated through face-to-face contact. Here it is necessary to communicate with consumers, events, messages about which get into the press and on TV, becoming a part of everyday life. The world's first brand of electrical goods, General Electric, was founded in 1892, Mercedes-Benz in 1885, and Remi Martin cognac in 1724.

As a rule, brand creation is a long and detailed work. Reputation is usually not immediately gained. Wal-Mart started slowly, using traditional small-town PR technologies: carnivals and parades with orchestras, poetry contests, and lullabies. But Volvo, which was the first to install seat belts in 1959, even now enjoys the reputation of being the safest and most reliable model.

PR, unlike advertising, is designed for long-term impact. No amount of creative and aggressive advertising of Western brands has displaced habitual brands of food products and cigarettes among consumers. As a result, new manufacturers were forced to adapt to these old brands.

In its most general form, the PR branding strategy is pretty simple.

- Creation of news, events with your product that arouses public and media interest.
- Do not rush, do not force events; it is better to gradually become an indisputable fact of being than to burn out as a one-day thing.
- Careful work with staff because it is he who is the face and voice of the brand for consumers.
- Come up with a new name.

Only after that you can and should think about advertising. Advertising is necessary for a brand, as its insurance and a reminder of it. Coca-Cola ads do not so much attract new consumers as reinforce old ones as if confirming their complacency: "You are great! You are doing everything right! "The best advertising projects are organized according to the principle: "I knew that, but it's good that you reminded me."

The most crucial strategic setting of branding positioning is perception management, changing the attitude towards a product (project, action, object, manager) without changing their real essence.

This attitude cannot in any way qualify as a deception: we are talking only about long-term trends in the development of the market environment, when "love" and "dislike" for a product is formed not so much through the declaration of its new characteristics (product positioning), but due to more or less successful branding positioning.

Moreover, in a market with a choice, let alone a wide and voluntary choice, perception is not an ersatz of reality but actually completely merges with it and even surpasses it. It should be noted that it is just right to offer, approximately, the following formula: perception is more than reality, and the brand is more important than the product.

One way or another, the brand must be organic to the surrounding context; in other words, to be located in a subject, geographic, physiological, and other spaces associated with their subject matter.

# CHAPTER 14

## Branding Color Schemes

**M**any studies have shown that a person perceives color, and then he performs actions, be it purchases or a choice, in favor of any product. Colors affect the feelings and emotions of a person. According to studies, only 20% of colors are "absorbed" by the vision; the nervous system perceives the remaining 80%. It has been established that each color evokes associations at the subconscious level of a person. Color can evoke different emotions: to attract, repel, soothe, excite, and disturb. The psychology of the effect of color has the same effect on all people without exception. For example, entering a store, we are looking for a product based on an existing image in our head. If the goal is to buy a can of condensed milk, the eyes will involuntarily look for a white and blue flower combination.

When looking at a particular color, a person has a spontaneous association of the color and the image that is associated with it, which is why manufacturers spend a lot of money on testing and careful selection for their future colors.

### 14. The Hypothesis

Psychologists put forward a hypothesis about the influence of particular colors on the identification of goods with different categories. For example, colors such as black, white, blue, red, and gold are "expensive" colors. In the minds of the consumer, such colors are associated with the elite segment. Practice shows that

121

combinations of blue or black with gold are very often found in products of a high price range.

If we consider a brand of "consumer" consumption, for example, McDonald's, the combination of red and yellow is associated with a sense of fun, joy, and warmth. There are associations with green and blue colors. Usually, these colors are used to show freshness and naturalness.

But some colors are entirely undesirable for combination; such combinations can cause negative emotions in the consumer. Such combinations can be purple and orange, bright crimson and red, turquoise and green, etc.

As you know, all colors evoke many associations and have a psychological effect:

Red: passion, strength, confidence, aspiration, will.

It expresses vitality, nervous activity, all kinds of inclinations and aspirations to get results and achieve success, impulsiveness, the will to win, the greedy desire for everything that can contribute to the saturation of life. Red is chosen by people who are emotional, amorous, and sexy. Its symbolic meanings are very diverse and, at times, contradictory. Red symbolizes joy, beauty, love, and fullness of life, and on the other hand, it symbolizes hostility, revenge, war, and blood. Red has been associated with aggressiveness and sexual desires since ancient times; it also signifies power and greatness. Of all the colors that can be used in a logo or packaging, red has the most potent effect on the consumer's psyche. Such as "Coca-Cola," "Old Spice"

White: purity, innocence, lightness, the color of complete openness, readiness to perceive the world in all its diversity.

White represents unity and freedom, openness and equality, lightness, and sociability. However, if there is too much white, it can be associated with boredom, frustration, isolation, and detachment. Manufacturers often use white to emphasize lightness. Such as "Vogue," "KENT."

Black: hardness, solidity, wisdom, depth.

The black color is enigmatic and mysterious, attracts, and challenges. This color is refined and solemn; it personifies dignity and grace. An excess of black color leads to the dominance of malicious traits, such as depression, cruelty, destructiveness. Black goes well with most other colors. The combination of black and white looks stylish, graceful, and elegant, most often used by manufacturers of expensive perfume, haute couture clothing, jewelry. In a logo, packaging, or advertisement, black looks extremely solid and reliable. For example: "Hugo Boss," "Armani," "Carte Noire."

Silver: freedom, swiftness, modernity, illumination.

Color style and forward movement. The negative traits include duplicity, deceit, and non-responsibility. Silver attracts attention; it is the color of expensive things—examples: Samsung, Pepsi light.

Gold: luxury, wealth, desire to stand out.

This color emphasizes its choosiness. But at the same time, it is the color of pathology and distrust. The gold color is actively used in packaging design, such as Gold Mark.

Orange: cheerful, impulsive.

A symbol of movement and active life. This color increases appetite, warms, keeps you toned, and energizes. The cafe uses orange plates and decor in the interior because this increases appetite and stimulates additional food orders, for example, "Fanta."

Yellow is the color of life and the sun, energetic, creative, original, cheerful.

The color of openness and sociability stimulates the brain, attracts attention, and remains in memory longer than other colors. It is the color of autumn, the color of mature ears and wilting leaves, and the color of disease. Also, yellow indicates talkativeness, intolerance, absent-mindedness, and the desire to criticize. Example: "Maggi", "Lipton".

Green is eco-friendly, natural, clean, fresh, calm.

Green color has a healing, relaxing effect, soothes, relieves pain and fatigue, balances, embodies freshness, and naturalness. Green is the color of grass and leaves. Also, green has negative characteristics - selfishness and jealousy. By its characteristics, it is green, the least eye-fatiguing color. Examples: "Doctor Mom," "Ahmad"

Pink: friendly, kind, feminine, romantic.

An excellent assistant in the field of personal relationships: it strengthens feelings, makes people more attentive, affectionate, and empathetic. If there is a lot of this color, then he may speak of frivolity. Example: "Mary Kay"

Blue: devotion, eternity, loyalty, purity, calmness, a sense of satisfaction, relaxation, spiritual and intellectual life, diplomacy.

Blue means idealism, organization, and grit. This color is harmonious and carries inner strength; it calms and relieves stress. It helps to concentrate on the essentials. The blue color in the logo will immediately attract attention and, unlike red, will never cause negative emotions. For many peoples, blue symbolizes heaven and eternity. It can also symbolize kindness, constancy, disposition. Examples: "Nivea," "Clearasil"

Purple is extraordinary, independent, exotic, intelligent.

The color of inner concentration, the color of the mystery, and the color of the surprise. Purple is one of the hardest colors to perceive.

Brown: stability, reliability, comfort, earthiness, realism.

Brown is the color of tradition. The color of chocolate, cocoa, and coffee. Examples: "Henessy," "Dove"

Thus, knowing how color affects the human psyche, you can learn to control consumers' emotions and influence their choice in your favor.

## *14.2 Psychology of Color*

The psychology of color is a study that allows you to understand how a person is affected by a particular shade of a well-known color scheme. It has already been proven that this theory has been popular since the dawn of civilizations, and each nation has its interpretation of colors. There are general concepts that describe the color perception of numerous groups of people (the color of mourning), and there are also individual characteristics that affect the perception and change the behavior of a particular person (in red, I feel more confident, but in a room with green walls I fall asleep faster).

Whether the psychology of color exists and what colors mean, we will check it out in this section.

### The Meaning of Colors in Psychology

It is known that having studied the meaning of colors in psychology, one can learn to conclude a person, his preferences, and his character. Usually, an individual has several shades that are close to him, and therefore are found in the wardrobe, the interior of a house or apartment, and accessories.

Often, preferences change, and often this is due to a negative situation and a specific color. After an accident or a negative situation, a person rejects a previously favorite shade.

For example, a person has an accident in the car of his favorite red color. Most likely, his next car will not be red. Or a student failed her exam by wearing her favorite blue dress. Perhaps she will choose an outfit of a different shade for a retake.

One way or another, the chosen color can tell a lot to psychologists more often than others. Professional psychologists most often use the Max Luscher test, invented in the late 40s of the twentieth century. Its simplified version can be tested in a domestic environment using TV color settings.

If there is more red in the image, the person has an aggressive and emotional disposition. Suppose yellow shades prevail as a friendly optimist. The blue-green range speaks at the same time of insecurity and potential danger from a person. The screen's blue color claims that the one who watches it is lazy, agreeable, loves to eat and drink.

American psychologist B. Schwartz deduced a theory that his car's color can tell a lot about a person. Happy, fortunate, and life-loving people drive red and yellow cars. Greens are acquired by realists and lovers of all kinds of flora and fauna; in blue cars, you can find confident and self-sufficient people, but the owners of gray and silver cars love themselves and know their worth. Fathers of large families and exemplary family men buy brown cars.

However, there is a specific relationship between how a person feels morally and what color he prefers at the moment. For example, when people feel good and happy, they choose bright colors in clothes. People with feelings of sadness or guilt tend to prefer the colors gray and blue. Those who sense danger choose green shades. With increased nervous excitement, red becomes popular.

It is known that the color environment of a person is capable of influencing the subconscious. Skilled designers and business people apply this knowledge in the design of offices, meeting rooms, study rooms. Of course, it is necessary to consider the individual preferences of workers, but psychologists developed the general postulates.

So, the rooms where negotiations are held are recommended to be painted blue; this improves the quality of business conversation and contributes to cooperation contracts. But the saturated blue color is no longer suitable; it contributes to the dispersion of attention and dispersal of partners.

Color also matters in performance. In a combination of blue, green, and red tones, people improve productivity. Small areas of yellow color stimulate the development of ideology, improve employees' mood, and allow finding compromise solutions.

**Briefly About Other Colors**

In addition to the explanation at the beginning of this chapter, other colors can also describe people's psychological characteristics. For example, dreamers with strong intuition like orange, good-natured and loving natures prefer pink. Infantile and quickly suggested personalities have purple things in their arsenal: they help them feel support and support from outside. This color is also an indicator of the level of fatigue: the more you like purple, the more you are tired.

Currently, popular color schemes are typical in advertisements for goods and services. Premium products are usually accompanied by a range of blues, golds, reds, blacks, and whites. From time immemorial, these colors have been symbols of power and wealth, belonging to high society. Packaging designed in such a color scheme automatically attracts the customer's attention and increases the desire to buy.

The combination of red and yellow colors used by the popular fast-food chain symbolizes cheerfulness, warmth, and fun. Green, blue packaging emphasizes the freshness of the products.

Color in human psychology has received colossal importance. It allows you to express happiness, joy, sadness, sadness, focus on essential things, and learn to relax.

Anyone interested in how color affects people's character can learn to understand others without words and determine their personality type. Use colors to improve your well-being and quality of life; most importantly, your brand identity!

# CHAPTER 15

## Branding Culture

T hroughout the evolution of branding in world practice, several concepts of brand culture have changed due to firms' strategic development, each stage of which has formed particular guidelines for the emergence of a new generation of companies. Since the beginning of the 20th century, which marked the development of mass industrial production, the corporate culture gradually reflected different strategic guidelines in the organization of in-house management and the development of its brands.

1. The orientation of the branding culture of management towards economies of scale was inherent in companies in the post-war period. After World War II, the beginning of the economic recovery helped create consumer demand and allowed firms to expand production capacity. The production-oriented factory structure best suited the firms' needs, providing strategic economies of scale.

2. The orientation of the branding culture of management towards product quality characterized the next stage in the development of internal corporate management systems. In the 1950s. quality management mechanisms began to be actively implemented in Japanese companies. "Quality mugs" and "quality boxes" have become widely known. In world practice, the concept of total quality control has been developed.

3. The orientation of the branding culture of management on the creation of demand marked the next era in the development of in-house management systems. Since the late 1970s, firms increasingly

began to orient their intra-firm mechanisms to market demand, laying consumer expectations and preferences in production activities. During this period, "pulling" business strategies received exceptional development.

4. The orientation of the corporate culture of management towards mergers and acquisitions in firms' strategic activities began in the late 1980s. The increase in the company's market presence was achieved by acquiring assets of competing firms and partners. During this period, a new generation of conglomerates emerged, the pace of integration of which reached unprecedented levels.

5. The orientation of the branding culture of management towards reengineering as a strategic direction of development was used by those firms that, as a result of massive capital transformations, faced the problem of duplicating management functions. Such firms needed consolidation and a higher degree of integration of divisional activities. Appeared in the late 1980s - early 1990s, reengineering primarily contributed to administrative, organizational problems.

6. The orientation of management's branding culture towards the total capitalization of assets entered the sphere of entrepreneurship in the mid-1990s. Firms built in-house mechanisms based on consumer preferences and expectations. This focusing on business activity on the market needs largely determined the upward trend in assets and increased share prices. A new wave of mergers and acquisitions, the development of e-commerce, and customer relationship marketing (CRM) principles in brand asset management have contributed to the capitalization of companies.

7. The orientation of the branding culture of management towards the development of brands is a consistent continuation in in-house management's strategic development. Modern management systems are primarily focused on the development of brands and brand assets. According to the management concept of brand orientation, the

consumer's decision in favor of a particular product is based primarily on trust in the company and its brand and only then on the product's functional advantages and consumer properties.

## 15.1 Modern Brands

Modern brands have a significant influence on the development of branding culture. Brand personality rises to the level of general brand values, the formation of which is directed by all in-house mechanisms.

The branding culture's orientation towards creating brands is especially essential for large, centralized companies, which are characterized by high transaction costs in making management decisions. If management decisions are contradictory, and the brand's mission periodically changes, then employees, partners, and clients of the company, being in a state of uncertainty, may lose motivation along with loyalty. Therefore, companies strengthen their corporate values and implement them through a single corporate vision, mission, and company philosophy.

Example

For example, Starbucks is based on "high quality and personal service," French brand Tefal focuses its culture on engaging and consumer value creation "Your ideas are indispensable," McDonald's promises "family fun and children's party," Disneyland says: "We are working to ensure that adults and children spend more time together." Facebook's mission: "To empower people to communicate and make the world more open and united."

The brand mission and philosophy of the brand develop the company's internal culture, when, under the influence of the formed style of behavior and relationships of employees, specific approaches to business and attitude to society as a whole are developed. The

131

brand values shared by all company employees have a significant impact on its manifestation and development in the market.

## Brand Culture: Components and Features

An internal brand culture is a strategic tool for capitalizing a firm. Particularly acute is forming a corporate brand culture for companies that combine assets as a result of mergers and acquisitions. In practice, the consolidation of assets is accompanied by the fusion of corporate cultures, which are often initially based on different values and traditions. In such a situation, brand management tasks are reduced to the optimal combination of the best qualities of both cultures while eliminating their shortcomings.

In world branding practice, there are two types of brand cultures: integrated and differentiated.

An integrated culture is based primarily on the material elements of the organization, and, according to the cultural concept, there are three components:

- visible artifacts (uniform brand architecture, employee uniforms, office design);
- expressed values (a visible manifestation of collective beliefs and attitudes, management hierarchy, management);
- unconscious values (implicit assumptions and the ideology of the team).

This culture model can be changed through tangible changes: interior design changes, communication implementation, educational programs, and other similar means.

A differentiated model of branding culture is based on a holistic perception of intangible values. An influential differentiated culture makes a brand extremely valuable for consumers and out of reach of competitors, allowing it to move into the category of global value and turn into a particular religion for consumers and company employees.

Example

Examples include Microsoft, Calvin Klein, Disney, Virgin, Manchester United, and others. An open attitude towards life characterizes the Virgin brand because all the company employees adhere to this attitude towards life. People strive to work in companies like Virgin because they get the emotions and the motivation they expect; they willingly become carriers and conductors of their brand values.

Elements of brand culture. In practice, a brand's branding culture in a company is formed by many components, both tangible and intangible.

The organizational structure reflects tangible, formalized processes, including a management hierarchy, a management system, distribution of rights, responsibilities, duties, and essential competencies. It defines the role of each employee in the development of the brand.

Behavior includes the system of relationships in the company, reflecting employees' beliefs about the vision of the brand, which manifests itself in their operational and current activities.

The language of brand communication is one of the most essential elements shaping brand culture. A directive, asking, or inspiring tone is used depending on the management level and the characteristics of administrative and organizational relationships. The brand language of communication reflects the cultural status and shapes brand culture bearers' thinking and behavior. It determines the perception of messages by employees of the firm:

- Directive nature usually creates additional barriers to mutual understanding, requiring action from employees from a position of authority;
- Request messages are more effective and are used much more frequently, as they allow employees to feel like participants in the dialogue and their involvement in developing brands. Despite the fact that most of the "requests" are directive in nature, the language of such appeals is softer and can arouse the employee's disposition;
- Inspirational messages are the most powerful type of communication in terms of motivation. This communication style gives the employee an emotional desire to achieve results and forms employee loyalty to the manager. Great politicians, coaches, and business people have proven through their examples that an inspiring approach can achieve incredible returns from even the smallest or most inexperienced teams.

Beliefs and attitudes represent the company's employees' fundamental assumptions about the world, the collective consciousness under the influence of which managerial decisions are made, and internal relations are formed between departments and individual specialists.

Traditions and rituals are structured processes, a kind of symbolic manifestation of culture in events and ceremonies. For example, it may be traditional to greet the manager with a bow, typical for Japanese companies, or the need to adhere to an individual style of clothing for employees. Also, brand traditions may include annual holidays for employee families or training seminars with visits to recreation areas.

## 15.2 The Formation of Brand Culture

The issues of brand culture formation are in the center of attention of specialists from various business areas, who adapt generally accepted principles to companies and industries' specifics. In particular, McKinsey specialists have developed the 7S system of brand values, seven elements of which form the culture:

1) Strategy: the main marketing strategy of the company in the market;

2) Structure: the organizational structure of the brand portfolio management of the company;

3) Systems: client databases and their management systems;

4) Style: a model or used approach to brand portfolio management;

5) Abilities: the professionalism and qualifications of specialists who develop brand values both within the company and in the external environment;

6) Employees: methods and mechanisms for motivating employees for brand development;

7) Shared values: the company's culture that determines the efficiency and innovation of all processes in the system of internal management and ensures the viability and development of brands.

The combined enhanced impact of all seven components on the firm's activities is of fundamental importance and provides a synergistic effect on corporate portfolio brands' development. Any change in the state of one of the seven factors dramatically changes the brand culture.

# CHAPTER 16

## Brand Differentiation and Brand Relevance

One of the main premises of branding is to generate differentiation. Find in companies or products what makes them different and put it in value. For every company, a necessary way to generate differentiation is the brand. In today's saturated market and with a hyper-informed public, the brand builds a vector that helps companies get closer to their audiences and establish who their favorites are.

But the differentiation itself doesn't make you relevant. Relevant does what you do for your audience. So if differentiation doesn't make me relevant, why do I have to work on it? Because to have the option of showing your audience if you are relevant or not, they must first know you, and for that, you have to stand out from the rest of the offers; stand out, differentiate yourself.

If you do not differentiate yourself, it is difficult for you to get a profitable and competitive business if you do not build your brand proposal. It doesn't matter if you are a neighborhood bakery or a large company; find your differential value, and build your brand proposition.

### 16.1 What Aspects Are Important to Work On to Build That Differentiation?

**The Product or Service**

The more differential the offer itself, the more possibilities there are to build a differentiating brand. This does not mean that you have to invent the wheel, but instead sell your product or service with drivers that are as differential as possible within the category. Let's think of a simple business, a bar; There are millions of bars, but some work better than others. It is easier to differentiate themselves from those who build their offer based on a differential aspect.

**The Value Proposition**

The promise you make to your audience because you are important to him. A phrase that connects the heart of your business with the heart of your target audience. The entire business strategy will pivot on this value proposition, and it is the basis for building a truly differentiating business. It has to be aligned with the aspects that motivate your audience (consumer insight)

**People**

People appears in third place but not because it occupies this place in the ranking of importance. They are a key element when we come into contact with a brand; it will largely depend on whether our experience is more or less satisfactory. How many times have you stopped buying somewhere because the people who attended you have not done it in the way you consider appropriate?

**Visual Identity**

The set of visual elements that "dress" your brand. Many times it is so differentiating that before seeing the brand, you already know who it is.

**Verbal Identity**

What you say defines you as much as your actions. This is an area that is often neglected and is as essential as all the others. Why do we get obsessed with colors and forget about words? If we decide that our business is characterized by being close or more formal, educational, or fun; All of this has to be consistent with your messages, and the words have to record it.

**The Brand Experience**

What do I live, how do I feel when I contact your brand? The brand experience is essential to generate notoriety and loyalty. We have infinite ways to satisfy the same need; that is why the concept of experience is becoming increasingly important for the user. If I want to buy shoes, I can do it through the web, and if I go to your store, it will be because you offer me something different.

Ultimately, these aspects are essential to building the differentiation of your brand; all this has to be consistent with the brand's personality and its value proposition. Don't forget that differentiation is the first step to relevance.

## 16.2 Brand Relevance Measurement

Brand relevance can be measured in many ways, but two are easily measurable Brand Salience and Top of Mind. Top of Mind refers to those brands or products that we remember within a specific category. For example, if they asked you for a brand of milk, which one would you say? The ones you mention first will be your top of mind. Brand Salience is the degree to which a brand is thought of during the buying process.

A marketing manager once told me that there were only three essential elements for his brand to be relevant: it had to be original, memorable, and relevant to many people. And it is that the relevance of a brand has to do with its orientation, such as having empathy with its target audience, speaking their language, understanding their needs and desires, and knowing what problem they have to solve it better than anyone else.

 What to do when a brand is no longer relevant and, therefore, no longer necessary for its users? What can you do about it? Depending on the case, some measures or others will be taken, but four simple keys lead to brand relevance:

## 1. Define the strategy

When the same people are in charge of a brand for years, it is very common to have a distorted version. In that moment comes inconsistency and incoherence. That is when it is to redefine itself. It is not necessary to change the course of your business drastically. You have to focus on the lines of action that help your business the most and put aside those that are out of date or are not relevant for your users.

## 2. Be up to date with the change in social customs

Identify those actions of your company that has lost its meaning due to social changes. We live in a society in which we need to express everything that we live or feel. It is a hypersensitive society that overreacts to stimuli and feelings. Do you think that your website, emails, social networks, etc. need some rework, and are you ready for it?

## 3. Change in lifestyle

Many organizations desire to connect with us in such a way that they are part of our lifestyle. Has the time come for a brand to understand society as it is and stop looking at it, judging it, or trying to change its behavior to accompany it? Is the time to stop selling to start relating? Our lifestyle has changed, but we are out if we do not renew the brand and its meanings. As simple as that.

## 4. Change in media consumption

If our social customs and lifestyles have changed, it was extraordinary to think that our way of communicating with people would not do it. Brands today have information about people like never before in history. Why then choose the less personal channels? Why be more arrogant than the statistics and decide not to change your email campaign or your cluttered promotional brochures if they don't work?

The survival of the brand depends on its relevance. And this requires constant study of the market, trends, and demographic changes. Brands that adapt prosper; those who don't adapt, regardless of their size or importance in the past, die because brands don't understand the size and attitude.

# CHAPTER 17

## Amazing Ways to Turn Customers to Fans with Your Brand

### 17.1 What Is Customer Love?

To show love for a client, you need to show concern and consideration. To do this, study your audience, find out what is missing, and give it. So you have a chance to make love mutual.

It is not easy to show love: you need to understand the pains and needs of people, show their importance, be sincere in your desire to help. It is much easier to sell a service with indifference. But you've to understand that your competitors will do the same. To become the best for your customer, exceed expectations: show interest, provide expert advice, and give gifts that they love.

Love is expressed in detail. So, personal congratulations on holiday can be a reason to fall in love with you. Some banks give birthdays a month of subscription to a site with serials and two online books. What did it cost them? Agree with partners, draw up a letter, and establish service. Winning a person's heart is priceless.

**Why Is It Important to Love Customers?**

People are becoming more demanding. Fast service or a pointless gift will no longer make you want to return. But the combination of good service and positive emotions is still addictive. Loved and loving clients become regular and acquaintances. This is what will help elevate your company.

It is important for a person to know what you want and can help. This is part of a long-term relationship. If you just sold the service, the client will give the money and not remember you again. To get the opposite effect, hone your skill in seduction: anticipate desires, get rid of problems, make life better. Grateful people are more likely to ask for help again and forgive the accidental slip.

## How Can You Show Love?

A sincere expression of love is not high-flown words but rather concrete actions. People can be charmed through the lens of attention to detail. Here's what you can do.

Show respect in any situation. Love your customers, even when they are hostile. Your goal is to fix this, so be careful about the reason. Don't make excuses or argue in response to negative feedback. Thank you for it, solve the problem, and make a gift. Be sincere in your desire to lift a person's mood; this will set you apart from those who cannot tame their ego.

Learn to listen and hear. Become someone to talk to, and you will have the opportunity to know the client better. Learn about the needs of the first person, conduct surveys and questionnaires, ask questions personally. This will help you find an individual approach to clients and create a competitive advantage.

This is what Carl Sewell, the owner of one of the finest auto dealerships in the United States and author of Customers for Life, did. He asked clients why they don't like going to auto centers. The clients found it inconvenient to work from 8 am to 3 pm, the workers seemed rude, and the prospect of being left without a car during the repair was very depressing. Karl was able to correct these shortcomings and created a competitive advantage for his company.

## Are There Any More Ways?

Build a team that wants to help people as passionately as you do. Train them, motivate, and inspire them with the desire to be the best for the client. Remember, if employees are eager to help, the spark from this fire can ignite the hearts of those who turn to them.

Be open and loyal. If your client is in a critical situation and you can solve his problem, do it for free. Your costs will pay off when the person contacts again. If you are contacted with an unusual request, determine how you can help.

Help develop and develop yourself. Produce educational content: host conferences, shoot video tutorials, write helpful articles. Determine what topics your audience is interested in and try to cover them in clear language. This will help people see the value in the knowledge that you give, and they may want to share it.

Promise less than you do. This way, you are less likely to disappoint the person who contacted you. For example, if your company delivers food, you can declare the delivery time with a margin of 15-20 minutes. When you bring dinner earlier, the client will be pleasantly surprised. And if you can't, you won't be upset. This system is easy to apply in different service areas.

So How Do You Make Your Customers Fall in Love with You?

We can only give what we have. To give love to customers and receive it in return, you need to love yourself and your business. Find the courage to make your dream work come true. The passion you will surrender to him will serve as fuel for moving towards goals, and the path itself will already be a reward.

Steve Jobs spoke about love for his work this way: "Understand yourself and understand what you love. It has as much to do with your job as it does with your personal life. Work will take up most of your life, and the only path to self-esteem is to do what you think is worth the effort. And the only way to do this kind of work is to love what you are doing.

Remember the benefits that you bring to the world and multiply them. By changing people's lives, even if only slightly, you will feel the return from them. This will help you get enthusiastic about new things and make your customers fans.

## 17.2 The Secrets of "Fanocracy."

American business strategist David Mirman Scott writes about this in the book "Fanocracy." He offers several ideas on how to do this. We selected the most interesting ones.

### #1. Surprise and challenge

American lingerie brand MeUndies offers customers a subscription to panties and unexpected prints. It would seem that this is too simple to become a fan of a brand, and there are many lingerie manufacturers in the world.

But MeUndies offers to choose the type of pattern; "classic", "bold" and "adventure", subscribe and automatically receive new underwear with a cool print every month, for example, "astronaut", "penguin party", "Candy Corn toffee". Interest is fueled by the fact that some models are available only to subscribers.

The brand slogan: "We have already dressed 9 million happy asses, but we are not stopping!" This unusual approach, coupled with good product quality, has created a large fan base around MeUndies.

### # 2. Get involved in the fan environment

The hangout of retro car lovers is massive and friendly, plus there are real car fans in it. The CEO of the insurance company Hagerty

Insurance Agency understood this. Therefore, he decided: it is necessary to establish a connection with this circle of people, to join the atmosphere, and to show that his company is also "in the subject." After all, this is a large market for potential customers.

Therefore, Hagerty Insurance Agency employees constantly go to auto shows. The company launched a service to evaluate vintage cars, teach young people to judge at retro car shows, and even created a free app for auto auctions. She also opened the Hagerty Drivers Club, whose members receive many "goodies" from a subscription to a thematic magazine to discounts on different salons' maintenance.

So the insurance company became part of the fanatic process around retro cars. And lovers of such cars have respected this company, recognized it as "their own" and insure their cars through it - not only old but also new, everyday ones.

If your product can somehow be associated with fan organizations, join them, and become "yours." Build your business around something that brings people together.

# # 3. Build a community around you

The legendary American bookstore Brookline Booksmith, unlike many other bookstores, is still thriving. This is because it does not just sell books, but for decades they hold literary discussions and organize hundreds of presentations, including the Booker and Nobel Prize winners.

While books are often bought online because of discounts, Brookline Booksmith customers are even willing to overpay. They come to the store, not for a budget purchase but for emotions and advice. Here they can chat about books, learn about new products, or meet the author. And behind the counter is the store owner, who himself is a fan of books and can advise something in a friendly way.

This is how a community of people has formed around Brookline Booksmith, who only go to this bookstore and take their friends there. These are the fans of the brand.

To create such a community, you need a genuine interest in customers' needs and interests, not just a desire to sell more, David Mirman Scott believes.

### #4. Broadcast values

Josh Murray from Australia started Josh's Rainbow Eggs. They cost nearly double as much as the competition and are still bought. Moreover, many customers exclusively prefer the eggs of this brand.

The fact is that Josh declares: on his farm, chickens walk freely; they are cared for, looked after, and given a lot of space. The entrepreneur calls his products "ethical eggs". Once he realized: many people are willing to pay for a produced product without bullying animals. And it worked: his brand had real fans.

### #five. Take slang names

One day, Adobe Systems decided to teach its fans how to mention their brand correctly. The company wrote right on the official website that it was correct to write: "the photo was processed using the Adobe Photoshop® program," but incorrectly, "we photoshopped the photo" and gave several other similar examples.

The artists and photographers who use the program were outraged and laughed. They shared a link to this set of rules on social media for a long time and wrote angry comments.

This is fundamentally the wrong brand policy, writes the author of the book "Fanocracy". When a "slang" name clings to a brand, it means "went to the people." This should be promoted, not suppressed. When people call the iPhone an "apple phone," it's a brand compliment, not an insult. Only unknown brands are called exclusively by the full name.

# # 6. Give an unforgettable experience

Grain Surfboards is a surfboard company. To separate themselves from competitors, they decided to sell finished products and kits for the board's self-creation. It includes tools and a piece of wood.

The surfboard is an exceptional item, so they were happy to buy these sets. But creating a board is a complicated process, which is why many people had questions. As a result, the company began to conduct master classes on the production of surfboards every month.

Fans can come to the city of York (USA) and, over several days, together with Grain Surfboards specialists, make their board. And then try it out at Long Sands Beach. They communicate with the same surfers and employees of the company, share stories, and learn more about the inner "kitchen" of Grain Surfboards.

When you give your fans something special, they have an experience that will last a lifetime. This is how they become brand ambassadors and their "walking advertisement."

# # 7. Do not lie

A company that uses primitive marketing tricks will never win over an army of fans. The key feeling to inspire brand fans is trust. If you try to deceive them, nothing will work.

Here are some typical marketing scams:

"Hurry up to buy! The product is already running out!" (not really)

"This is the best price! It won't be cheaper!" (but such discounts are often)

"Due to the large number of calls, you will have to wait longer on the line" (but you always have to wait a very long time)

In 2018, the International House of Pancakes (known in America as IHOP) announced that they were changing their name to IHOb. The company even tweeted a photo of it changing the sign. The brand said: what the letter "b" means, they will report in 2 days.

All this time, fans of the brand discussed social networks that the letter "b" means. Many people thought it was about burgers. Even The Washington Post and CNN wrote about the name change of the famous brand. And on that day, the company said they were joking and did it just to get attention. The brand wanted more social media to talk about the fact that they have on sale, not only pancakes but also burgers. Instead of the expected smile and ad, the brand received huge fan disappointment and hate. Nobody likes to be deceived.

# CHAPTER 18

## Branding Using Your Name

A brand cannot exist without a name: the name is the beginning of a success story. And how do you find the name for a brand?

Give someone or something a name. If you think about it, sooner or later, we all have to do it. What fun! Or ... what effort?

When we have to find a name for a company or a product, in short, projects bigger than us, which will also involve other people, yes, things get complicated. The choice must be well thought out and take into account many elements.

The time has come to explore the subject together.

The set of all the activities necessary to find names that make sell—commercial names for small and large companies and individual products or services. To make brand naming, you need to focus only on the verbal aspect of the brand, considering everything related to the definition of a commercial name. To work correctly and flawlessly, it is essential to know these three disciplines:

1. The semiotics (the science that studies sign) and linguistics

2. The marketing

3. The intellectual property (the laws that protect inventiveness and creativity)

Can you find the perfect name for your project? Studying the process in detail, we explain how in this chapter! And by supporting the creative phase with adequate research, you will indeed have good ideas. First, however, we must delve into the brand name's concept together to proceed without hesitation.

The brand name, which is the brand's name, is the ultimate goal of brand naming activities. It serves to "give an identity, to evoke the values of a company, to generate a sensation, to make a company or a product recognizable, unique, memorable, and repeatable. If you think about it, the names evoke completely different images, sensations, and emotions.

Have you ever wondered why? Phonetics has something to do with it. Names are words formed by letters which, pronounced individually or next to each other, give rise to particular sounds. The sounds of vowels and consonants convey precise meanings in all languages: for example, the "A" opening and welcoming, the "U" on the contrary closing, the "C" hardness, the "M" affection and love. Names are primarily phonetic.

The brand name is a word with specific phonetic characteristics that has become a name, around which a world, an experience, is then built. The name supported by a communication strategy becomes a brand name; otherwise, only a word remains.

The name is primary and essential for the brand (or company, product, or service): a brand cannot exist without a name. The name is the beginning of a success story; the name is the memory of the brand. The name lasts over time think of names like Fiat; the brand name is the brand's perpetually updated synthesis.

At this point, perhaps, you are wondering if brand names are all the same or if there is a way to select the strongest ones for your target market. Good question: let's answer by making the first distinction.

Descriptive brand name vs. a distinctive brand name

Think about the descriptive brand names, you know. Imagine placing them on a line with two ends: the generic character on one side, the badge on the other. Each brand name would occupy a specific position. On the one hand, there are descriptive names close to the generic character; on the other hand, the distinctive names recall different semantic universes.

Which are the strongest? Let's compare them.

The descriptive names:

- denote little personality
- they need a budget to spend on advertising to emerge
- are not enforceable from a legal standpoint
- they do run the risk of losing the right if they become common
- The distinctive names:
- have a substantial impact
- can be made memorable with communication
- are legally protectable

It is no coincidence that the prominent successful brand names worldwide are distinctive, not descriptive. Describing limits and prevents the name from evolving. It is also true that from a strategic point of view, a company can decide to focus on a descriptive name.

However, when you deal with brand naming, always remember that its meaning is entirely irrelevant; most people don't know or don't remember its meaning. What matters is the world of values that the brand evokes thanks to the name, through communication.

When a company or a product is born, everything starts from the name. Do you remember? We identified it a little while ago: the name is the beginning of the story. Everything starts from there; then comes the logo, a figure that treats the brand name with graphic elements and the payoff, a synthetic and expressive formula that completes the name.

Don't make the mistake of thinking that the brand can exist without a name. It is not so. Graphic designers do an essential job on the logo, it is true, but it is you in the first place with the name that gives life to the brand. The name has a discreet and absolute strength, without even fulfilling the task of describing (the description is partly the payoff task).

## How Is Brand Naming Done?

Now that you know more about brand naming let's move on to the operational phase.

First of all, your brand naming strategy must take into account the seven main tasks of the brand name; be prepared to find a name that meets these requirements:

1. identify the company's commercial proposal

2. differentiate from the competition

3. uniquely personalize the company's offer

4. communicate with the public by creating a relationship

5. retain the customer

6. protect against counterfeiting

7. capitalize on the investment made in the brand

Before you jump into creative brainstorming, you need to internalize the seven brand name tasks. You must be aware that creativity is fundamental, and at the same time, "forced" within impassable boundaries.

## Methods for Choosing the Brand Name

Have you ever heard of Naming Circle? It is a schematic model that leaves nothing to chance in the generation of different brand name proposals.

The Naming Circle foresees that, together with creativity, three essential aspects come into play: linguistics, marketing, and individual ownership - yes, remember well: we also listed them in the opening paragraph of the article. Let's see them one by one.

### Linguistics

The linguistic approach allows us to evaluate brand name ideas based on the name's pronounceability, memorability, and exportability.

The name in question must be easy to pronounce not to alienate the consumer or the relevant public; moreover, its reading must also be verified for similarity concerning other names in the markets where it could be exported. Ultimately, the name must be easy to remember.

Okay, we recommend that you prepare a checklist to tick as you go through the verification.

### Marketing

Brand name proposals acquire value if they take into account marketing and, in particular, brand identity. This approach highlights the names' consistency with the brand or product's positioning, the company philosophy, the public, and the reference sector.

Please do not fall into the trap of proposing names linked to the fashions of the moment; on the contrary, do a thorough analysis of the brand personality to understand how direction it is going and find ideas that can adapt to the evolution of the markets. A wrong name can be costly: it can limit sales and is difficult to change.

## Intellectual Property

Each brand name proposal must first be verified and then legally protected. The brand name must be free, original, and defensible: there are websites where it is possible to do a preliminary search, also through a match with the product classes of membership. It is good to know that only "well-known" brands, for example, Champagne, prevail over all product categories even if they are not legally registered and protected in all classes of products and services.

The legal approach in choosing a name also includes other precautions that should not be overlooked. The brand must not be misleading with respect to what it represents; that is, it cannot declare false things; the trademark must be lawful and cannot use offensive words on the product market.

Please make sure the names you devise can be protected, especially since they only belong to one owner. Do an in-depth search within the product classes, only present proposals for truly defensible brand names.

Thus, we provide you with a helpful four-step scheme, which presents a practical technique for generating a brand name. This technique is invaluable for working on the verbal aspect and finding names without graphics and logos.

It develops in four phases.

1. Define, clarify the need. What should the name express, and how should it express it? These aspects need to be clarified already during the first meeting.

2. Explore creativity. Creation and selection are incompatible: in this phase, the mind must be free to "travel" without evaluating. Synonyms, neologisms, fictional names must be explored in groups or individually, even using computer media.

3. Select. What are the best proposals that emerged during the creative phase? The screening of names must be based on linguistic and marketing criteria.

4. Check. Legal research concludes the process: verification must be carried out on the (at least) five strongest proposals, also supported by a survey with consumers. It is useless to present brand name ideas that have not been legally verified.

# CHAPTER 19

## Common Brand Challenges

Over the past few years, everyone has tried to make their brands successful. Making people talk about themselves, "reaching out" to the consumer, making their brand "advanced," everything has been tried. In this movement's vanguard were the now-long-lived Internet enterprises, guided by the idea that endless investments in communication with the consumer will help create a successful brand. The "eruption" of brands left behind many undermined brands, weakened or strayed from the right path. Listed below are nine common brand health complaints and suggestions for first aid.

### 19.1 Brand Challenges

1. I know my brand is in decline, but I don't know why.

There are several reasons for this. Suddenly, brand positioning that seemed so simple and straightforward becomes vague and incomprehensible. Unfortunately, when this happens, many companies take rash steps: changing advertising agencies, firing marketing directors, holding urgent meetings, and expecting the company's president to have a brilliant saving idea. Some argue that you need to spend more, others that less. Everyone has an opinion. But the problem is that any opinion is just an opinion.

If you can't tell exactly why your brand has fallen into disrepair, you need to understand it. Start with an almost anthropological approach, which I compare to large-scale excavation: go back to the brand's origins. What was his original image? Why did he then resonate in the hearts of buyers? What were its core values? Have they survived? And just as importantly, have they retained the same meaning? The world is changing, and you need accurate data. Conduct consumer research on products in your category. What do they think of your competitors? What does your product or service give them? What are its material benefits, and perhaps more importantly, what are its emotional benefits? Imagine this is some "audit" of the brand, and don't let your personal bias influence the process. Listen and conclude.

2. My brand direction changes with every new product and marketing campaign. There is neither consistency nor purposefulness in its development. How to deal with this?

Think like Plato! This great Greek philosopher may not be called an outstanding marketer, but he understood the basic principle on which any successful brand is based: the concept of essence. Plato believed that in anything, the idea of this thing is hidden. In other words, Plato was the first to express the importance of the essence of the brand. For example, the Nike brand's essence is "For real sport" (authentic athletic performance). When everyone in the company understands what the phrase means, employees can innovate in all aspects of business, from advertising and product design to promotions. All of this leads to larger and more lasting results.

3. I have a boring brand. Consumers and employees alike are indifferent to him (not to mention Wall Street).

Maybe your brand can use a little "psychotherapy."

Abraham Maslow, the founder of humanistic philosophy, is not often cited among the best marketing figures in history. However, Maslow's idea of human motivation is his "hierarchy of human needs," placing complex needs above basic survival needs holds the key to any brand's future. Because of the abundance of products and services on the market, it is not enough to have brand awareness or a superficial connection between the brand and the consumer. Brands need to connect with consumers on a deeper psychological level. They must acknowledge and respect the consumer's emotions, feelings such as the desire for belonging, the need for connection, the hope to overcome, and the desire to experience joy and achieve self-actualization.

Discerning companies recognize that successful products and services are profitable and help improve lives in some way. This understanding is at the heart of expressing the Starbucks brand. Regarding the Starbucks "massive digs", experts discovered the role coffee has played in society for over 500 years. And also discovered that coffee is not just a drink but a sensation that has been part of our culture for centuries. It was on this basis that the expression of the essence of the brand was built. For Starbucks, it is essential not to offer the consumer a cup of excellent coffee to offer him/her to enjoy the process of drinking coffee. So experts need to move to a higher level of Maslow's pyramid and found that we were thinking about more than just a cup of coffee.

4. My brand is dead

And it happens. You have ignored the brand for too long or let its development take its course, and one day it expired, losing all the energy and ability to captivate the imagination of your customers and yourself.

But there is also a positive side in this situation: even a dead brand can be revived or wholly transformed. For example, Banana Republic; at first, it was a clothing company that came up with a "zest" for itself: it is more interesting to buy safari-style clothes in a store decorated with artificial palms, packing boxes, and jeep parts.

This attracted buyer for a while. But the life of even the most beautiful but narrow concept is too short, and this version of the Banana Republic was soon threatened with extinction. Nevertheless, there was something about the brand, some elements in the concept of "everyday business wear" that could revive it. The company GAP acquired the Banana Republic and transformed the brand into a higher-end retailer offering a range of products from simple sweaters to aromatherapy products and Donna Karan-inspired crepe suits. This transformation was a huge step forward and the rebirth of the brand. (Of course, a new transformation will be needed over time).

5. My brand lives in the past

This happens with the best brands. With the best brands, they almost always happen: they take off like a comet, reach a certain level, and not go any higher. It's not enough the incremental improvements they are doing; transformation is needed.

This happened to Nike. In 1987, it was trying to move beyond its narrow customer base of dedicated male athletes and reach a broader audience. Until then, the Nike brand was all about competition: the brand's DNA was riddled with testosterone, and its character could be summed up as "please don't contact the wimps." The phrase "For real sports" ("Authentic athletic performance") was understood too narrowly. Nike needed to shift from "exclusion" of consumers to "inclusion." Simultaneously, it was impossible to alienate the audience of those young men who considered Nike "their" brand.

A few months later, they aired a TV spot called Revolution, which was radically different from anything the company had done before. It was a complex interweaving of black and white images captured on 8mm film that spanned various cultural phenomena. The ad's idea was that the Nike brand appeals to both women and men, old and young, unknown amateur athletes and world champions.

The problem was that the ensuing campaign went down the wrong path. The Hayward Field video, which featured the Oregon State University stadium treadmill, was directed inward and backward. They wasted ad time after previewing it to the thousands of Nike salespeople who walked away from the meeting with nothing to show to shoe buyers at the start of the new school year. They found themselves in a very challenging position. So they asked ad agency, Wieden + Kennedy, to go back to the beginning with a simple and straightforward task: stop talking and let consumers have access to the brand. The emotional and physical benefits of sports and physical activity were much broader than the definition.

Two weeks later, they received a response from Dan Weeden, David Kennedy, and four or five other agency employees (who then made up half of the agency's staff). Consumers already knew everything there was to know about the benefits of physical activity. Most of them were not happy with their physical condition, but they did not have time for serious sports. Why tell them these unpleasant facts again? They just needed to be encouraged and set the task in an optimistic spirit. "Just Do It" was a watershed moment for Nike, creating a broad communication platform that they could reach out to almost anyone. This phrase applied not only to sports at the level of world achievements but also to the fundamental human values shared by both triathletes and visitors to shopping centers. This phrase was not a product statement, either. She expressed the character of the brand. Nike has found a way to pay homage to the past while facing the future. "Just Do It" became the very expression of Nike's timeless values that the brand needed.

6. My brand is too narrow.

Here are five good ways to increase the "range" of your brand.

First, co-branding profitably with the right partner who will add value to the project you do not have. The Starbucks coffee brand deal with

United Airlines, which brought Starbucks coffee on United Airlines flights, enabled both parties to achieve their brands' essential goals.

Second: expanding the brand. There was a trendy section at the end of Time magazine about exciting people. The brand was expanded to create People magazine, which successfully expanded its brand: Teen People magazine. (Be extremely careful about brand expansion. An awkward "move" can ruin a new product and negatively affect the "parent")

Third: master new distribution channels. The presence of Starbucks coffee on United Airlines flights has become the co-branding of the coffee. And the distribution of whole-bean coffee and ground coffee through over 30,000 grocery stores created an additional channel for an existing product.

Fourth, master new product categories. For example, the range of Ralph Lauren paints that are now sold in hardware stores. The company discovered a new category and a new distribution channel.

Fifth: create a new sub-brand. Nike is a big brand, but Air Jordan is an incredibly successful sub-brand. Toyota is a big brand, and Lexus is such a successful sub-brand that most car buyers don't even perceive it as a sub-brand of the company that created it (this is perhaps the best compliment a sub-brand can give).

7. I have an immature brand.

Shortly before the collapse of the Internet enterprise, an expert gave a lecture to a group of executives from Silicon Valley. With great stock options and high hopes for the future of their young ventures, they wanted to learn how to make their newly created brands explosively successful. He told them to think like parents: building a successful brand is like raising a good child. This means you need to be patient. (Unfortunately, they wanted to hear something different).

Building a successful brand requires consistent management, long-term vision, and an unwavering commitment to brand values. Brands, like children, adopt the qualities of those who grow them. Like children, brands thrive best in an environment of inspiration, care, and learning where they are respected, protected, and understood. When building your brand, be consistent, and committed to your goal. Redeployment of branding responsibilities and management shifts in an organization can well lead to a problem brand. It takes a brand time to develop its values and personality. Those who are good at brand management, like good parents, instill in their brand's values that help them grow and be resilient. Profitable brands outlive their creators as children outgrow their parents.

8. My brand has dropped to the level of consumer goods.

If you ignore even a viable brand long enough, it can be reduced to the level of consumer goods—for example, coffee before Starbucks. Of course, before Starbucks, there were large coffee companies. Rather than delighting shoppers with the brand, these companies have worked hard to satisfy grocery chains. They saved wherever they could and stacked their produce in tall piles at the end of the aisles in the store. These stacks of green and red cans have transformed a formerly remarkable product into a commodity.

If this happened with your product, remember: you don't have to start hard and uselessly spend money. One of the lessons of the collapse of Internet businesses is that brand awareness is not equal to brand strength. Even the best advertising cannot create something that does not exist.

General advice: set yourself a high goal first. Good brand creators don't just transform a product; they act as champions of an entire category. That's what Nike has achieved with sneakers, Starbucks with coffee, and Southwest Airlines with flying.

162

Second, take your product to the next level. If you do not want it to remain a commodity item, offer a unique product that is so much better than the others, you cannot call it a commodity item. For example, is Krispy Kreme just donuts?

Third, offer more than the product itself. Create a specific atmosphere around him, paying attention to even the smallest details.

And fourth, remember that a company is a brand. Customers see your values behind the product and how you do business. Today, the difference between similar products may lie in the reputation of the manufacturer.

9. My brand is not advanced.

"Advanced" and "ahead of all" are dangerous words. Dan Weeden is right when he says to clients who want to be "ahead of everyone else," it's easy to go astray. In contrast to one view, Nike's goal is not to be "advanced," as the brand knows that "prowess" is determined by its customers, not by its headquarters employees. Be careful not to plinth the "advance". This is a false god.

Given the global trends, It's recommended that companies care more about their karma than about how to become "advanced." Our concern about the impact of globalization on cultures and the environment will only increase, and business conduct standards will rise. With this, we will expect the brands we trust the most to help bridge the enormous gap between profit and public benefit.

We are at the edge of the whole world of brands and are just beginning to see what issues and opportunities are associated with brand karma. However, it develops; I know that strong karma will develop if you do the right thing year after year: be honest, principled, and respect consumers, employees, and the environment. Companies like Nike and Starbucks are not perfect, but I am sure they will help write a new chapter on brand management, which already has a great need. They will prove that "big" does not necessarily mean "bad," that profits are only one measure of success, and that profitable brands can use their unique superhuman capabilities for good.

## 19.2 Your Brand in Times of Crisis

In times of economic crisis, it is even more important to remember the mission of a brand and its identity. When the market suffers from a problematic contingency, the games get tough, and it is in these circumstances, every little difficulty becomes an insurmountable obstacle.

Companies that in the past did not understand the centrality of the brand find themselves having to solve problems of a profound and various nature. The brand is like a "lifesaver", even if its quality and services are essential. Similarly, no one would deny the usefulness of advertising, but when you go through a widespread and deep-rooted economic recession, product and advertising become necessary but not sufficient.

People today don't just want to buy a product; they want to buy an idea that goes beyond the product; they need the Brand, with a capital B, which in this circumstance we can define as an elixir of pure emotional involvement. It is well known that market competition must be faced by clearly defining what a brand personifies. However, although this is a well-accepted assumption, few companies still invest in the evolution of their business from a mentality based on 'offer towards a strategy aimed at affirming the brand.

Business development

For a brand to perform its functions as a "business developer," it is vital that it is considered a living being, as if it were a person in flesh and blood, complete with brains and emotions. As such, the brand also grows and gains experiences over time; he must progress and act

164

promptly concerning his surroundings while remaining consistent with his personality. So, when the economic context puts a strain on individuals' optimism, discouraging consumption, and limiting purchasing power, it is often the brand that protects companies from bankruptcy and supports them to fight in difficult times. In extreme cases, survival is also considered a success.

Thanks to the brand, it is possible to enjoy privileges that the product has lost for a long time, such as entering less crowded strategic territories or the flawless attitude of capitalizing on every good deed performed in the past years. The brand is, in fact, an excellent catalyst of value and an excellent "business developer," always full of energy which, unless superhuman and repeated frontal attacks - feeds itself thanks to every single performance on the market.

Time to time

Everything ages, but we have learned that a brand kept under control needs fewer measures than the product, which instead, aging often dies inexorably. Like the proverbial long-life serum, a brand allows the company to slow down its pace in times of crisis and, if necessary, take a practical step towards its conservation, accusing lower risks of regression than a company not supported by the brand.

In these moments, a brand also fulfills the role of a "protective shield", using its ability to be noticed and distinguished on the market, giving the customer a reason for choice even in difficult times. A brand has the intrinsic function of communicating values and direct messages, building that credibility, essential in times of recession, reassuring the consumer, and facilitating the company's necessary marketing tactics. But the most vital thing about the brand is its ability to create solid relational and interactive relationships with its customers, satisfying the need for moral support indispensable to each individual, especially when there is that widespread social climate of collective pessimism.

# CHAPTER 20

## How to Effectively Communicate Brand Identity

T he channels and elements that help you convey your brand's values and personality in a targeted way. We experience it every day; communication is the basis of every interaction. Private life and the world of work: introducing yourself, interacting, and collaborating depend on the communication process.

When you showcase your business, you need to communicate who your brand is significant. Otherwise, you risk not getting the desired results. To improve communication with your audience and not fall into trivial mistakes, read our tips.

How to communicate the brand identity?

A brand identity is like a person's personality. The distinctive features of a character can also be found in the characteristics of a brand. We know how a person can make himself known; what happens to a brand? Everything starts with the communication of the brand identity.

Take advantage of these three aspects:

- Listen to your audience. Focus on the target audience and identify their real needs.
- Set up a strategy for your content. Use blogs and social pages to talk about your brand and products.

- Talk to your customers. Involve people actively, create a relationship of trust that leads to giving more prominence to the brand.

Brand-identity-authenticity

## Develop communication: web channels

Before communicating the brand identity, you must have a brand identity. If you have not yet clarified all the elements, you can find several ideas in this guide. If, on the other hand, the brand identity is clear and defined, you are ready to go and develop communication.

Brand-identity-communication-online

## Website and social network

Your online communication's basic idea is to show your company's principles and ideas in a clear, immediate, and consistent way. When designing your website, consider the characteristics that a right portal must have, including immediacy, usability, valid content, and the study of keywords that can help in SEO. Be careful to choose relevant keywords, which immediately indicate the identity of the brand. Thanks to the site, the brand identity can shine through from the visual aspect, with reference to the colors and the brand logo, and obviously through the contents, as discussed in previous chapters.

Texts, images, videos; all the material present must be aligned with your brand's tone of voice and attitude. Taking care of this aspect serves to reach the public immediately, transmit trust, and be recognized. To reinforce the work, you do on the site, activate the company social pages.

Always keep the target as a reference and establish which social networks to be present on; based on the audience type, a social channel will be more effective.

As the website does, so social networks talk about your company, promote your products, and reach customers; they speak more directly and conversely, but always respecting the brand's tone of voice. Combine these tools with your brand identity, creativity, and the value of your products, and that's it.

## Visual Marketing

On the web, communication passes more and more through images; you cannot underestimate this aspect. Part of the expression of the brand identity is related to the visual aspect.

The logo, photos, and videos, or more simply the use of colors, make the difference in determining a brand's success. Use it to impress people. The different techniques you can use to express your brand are coordinated through visual marketing.

This is precisely the strategy you develop visually to attract and engage your customers. In short, it represents the heart of the videos, gifs, and drawings, and photographs you use to represent your brand. Visual marketing is a powerful tool to guide the customer and direct him to purchase and remain etched in his mind.

## Elements for Effective Communication

Anyone can find it challenging to speak in front of new people, mostly fearing that they will make a wrong impression. This unlikely hypothesis could also strike when you try to communicate your brand.

To avoid it with ease, set some guidelines. Find them below:

## Be authentic

Conveying the authenticity of your brand is essential.

We are used to recognizing people for their character traits, how they behave, and their look; the same happens when we interact with a brand. In short, clearly expressing the distinctive traits and values of a brand and its authentic trait helps to be remembered.

Also, changed the aesthetic part; perhaps of your packaging, people will still identify the brand. The basis of authenticity will create a common thread between brand identity and customers' daily interaction with your brand.

## Focus On Quality

The quality is a must; in all you do. In this context, a brand identity is a tool that helps you present your brand. And it does so by speaking of quality, of course, but also by exploiting it. What do you mean?

Simple, demonstrating that even in the aspects that define the brand identity, the value is not lacking. The contents, graphics, videos, advertising, everything must be taken care of and convey the efficiency with which you work.

## Use storytelling

We are curious; we like to discover the news and be informed about the facts. For this reason, storytelling has taken hold more and over the years: it is about talking about a story, using images and concepts already known to the listener, to create an atmosphere of sharing and involve him. It constitutes a strong link with the public, capturing the attention and binding the customer to the brand. By leveraging emotions and feelings, interactions with customers will be increasingly reliable and lasting.

## Give your opinion

We just said we are curious people; we like to know what others are saying and thinking. That's why expressing your ideas and giving your perspective allows you to communicate the brand's identity powerfully. You have to speak for the brand, so remember to challenge customers in this direction. Blogs, posts on social media, forums: take advantage of all the media to promote your content by supporting it with topics in line with the brand values.

**Relate to The Public**

When your brand talks to customers, it can take different approaches. In defining the brand identity, you have already evaluated the tone of voice that distinguishes the brand, so you can experiment with different ways to build relationships with buyers.

Let's take some examples:

The humor. In the right doses, focusing on irony brings numerous advantages. First of all, it gives a lively and cheerful idea of the brand, which will be more easily remembered. Attracts attention and creates immediate contact with the reader, also stimulating conversation, given the spontaneous reaction's immediacy to something funny.

Nostalgia. Take a step back in time if you want to excite people. Take into account the target audience's context and interests, then ask yourself which memories they may be most connected to.

Finally, work on content to recall some detail or event from the past that can be linked to your brand.

The provocation: Allow yourself some excess and launch some provocation that breaks the habit. A little bit out of the box content makes a significant impact and can make your brand stand out. But be careful; exaggerations must be avoided to avoid negative repercussions on your brand identity.

An experiment in front of an audience. You never know what will work. Analysis and research on the target give you ideas and guidelines, but it may not be enough. So what to do?

Our suggestion is twofold: don't get stuck on a single strategy, but experiment with multiple paths. Try one thing at a time and evaluate the effects; finding the right key to communicate your brand identity takes time. So don't be discouraged and keep looking for new solutions all the time.

The personality of your brand and your content must move together. On the one hand, showing the brand identity in your material makes everything more incisive. On the other hand, content that aligns with the brand's character improves interactions with the public and increases popularity. In short, the two aspects work together to strengthen the positive perception of your brand.

# CHAPTER 21

## The First Product to Sell Is Your Brand

Only through a strong brand, with its well-recognized values and meanings, is it possible to stand out in a landscape characterized by the diversity of competitors and the fragmentation of the means of communication. To obtain this differentiating result, it is necessary to have a solid brand identity, which refers to that set of visual, textual, and verbal with strategic objectives. They have the task of making the broadcaster recognizable and building differentiating memorization.

This definition helps to understand how brand identity, rather than a question of communication, relates to the company's business. Brand identity is often associated with the need to promote the final image that the company would like to project on the market. Still, it is a mistake because brand identity should not be confused with advertising, is of its disciplinary autonomy. As such, it must be strategically grafted; that is, it must be born from the business idea that moves the company and then develop consistently concerning everything that the brand intends to declare to the market and its customers.

### 21.1 Branding, A Competitive Lever to Differentiate Yourself

To fully understand the importance of brand identity in determining the success or failure of a brand, it is useful to start from a general consideration: in the global world in which we live, almost all major consumer goods and products are easily cloned and reproducible, and increasingly rarely constitute the real element of competitive differentiation in the business market. To be clear, we do not buy a certain car just because it is a means of transport, or a certain food only to nourish us, or even a dress to protect us from the cold; we choose them for what they represent, for the values and meanings they carry.

However, given that a substantial homologation of the offer characterizes each product sector, then the main game to conquer the consumer is played on the terrain of the brand, understood as that conceptual entity that presiding over the mental territory of individuals, it evokes a set of predefined values, thus defining the positioning on the market.

From this point of view, branding's strategic value is clearly understood and a discipline responsible for the creation and construction of the brand and a business approach to the market, based on a strategy aimed at selling a brand, not the only product.

So branding is configured as the competitive lever capable of allowing the construction of a single proposal, this yes, unlike products, which are difficult to duplicate: think, for example, of the added value that consumers generally attribute to the iPod of Apple, compared to other mp3s out there.

So branding will configure a particular way of doing business in which the centrality of the brand is enhanced as a strategic asset of the company, outlining how the company organizes itself and proposes itself on the market.

## 21.2 Brand identity, communication compass

However, suppose it is true that brand identity should not be confused with communication because it must unfold 'upstream' together with the business idea, in the relationship with fundamental variables such as the market scenario and the competitive landscape in which the company is located. In that case, it is also true that the link with the dimension of communication is very strong because the latter is strongly influenced by brand identity.

In particular, without an adequate and preliminary definition and understanding of the brand's distinctive features to study a brand identity, any subsequent communication action would inexorably risk losing effectiveness, risking not being consistent with the values and meanings decided by the identity strategy.

Consequently, it is therefore well established that advertising and all other forms of communication must be consistent with the main 'visual codes', characterized by specific colors, a particular iconography or typeface, 'text codes', such as a name, a payoff, or a message to be transmitted, and the 'evocative codes', which refer to a symbolic world to be transmitted and the sensations to be communicated.

Otherwise, if this were not the case, there would be a risk of reducing the performance value of the communication activated, and ultimately of wasting the budget invested. In this discourse, every form of communication should be an expression of brand communication, i.e., an initiative focused not so much and not only on the company's products and services but committed to communicating the brand itself, with its essential identity background.

Moreover, we hear a distinction between product communication and institutional communication, while brand communication has a transversal value and should permeate every form of activated communication.

But be careful, very often, there is a tendency to reduce the brand identity to the visual identity of the brand, making a subtle mistake of simplification: because the identity of the brand is not given only by 'what you see, i.e., by brand design but also from 'what you read' and 'what you hear'. Companies turn to agencies in our sector only for the choice of the logo, the typeface, the chromatic identity, and the iconographic system, but the brand identity cannot be summarized only in these aesthetic outputs; there is also a cultural component as we have been explaining in this guide.

## The Value Heritage of the Brand and The Point of View of Consumers

Another fundamental element to be considered to understand the dynamics of branding is undoubtedly the brand equity, which we can translate as the value heritage of the brand and represents the set of values that the brand decides to bear. In particular, the wake of brand equity represents the set of distinctive and differentiating values with which a brand presides over the individual's mental territory, thanks to which it places itself and competes on the market.

It is thus becoming the founding link of a modern business strategy. In other words, brand equity is everything that should be told to the public if, when promoting a product, we were not allowed to say anything about the product itself. But not to be overlooked is the brand image, which, corresponding to what consumers think of a particular brand, is the fundamental variable to be considered when intervening on an existing brand's brand identity.

It is, in fact, evidence that the detection of substantial inconsistencies between the brand image perceived by consumers and the brand identity issued by the company would indicate the presence of structural problems and errors, to be corrected with a right remodeling of the brand identity, which should involve all the company management and not just the marketing department, as usually happens.

The ethical approach? A necessity, but consistency is needed.

Eventually, an increasingly central theme that influences the construction and remodeling of the brand identity is undoubtedly ethical. Today, thanks to the transformations produced by the internet and social media, companies find themselves in the position of having lost the monopoly of controlling the communication process.

In a context in which the recipients have also become the issuers of messages and information content, brands find themselves under constant observation and evaluation. This means that if a brand does something wrong, it exposes itself to public and collective criticism more quickly than in the past.

So, how to behave? The first rule to follow is to avoid improvisation, in the sense that ethical approaches must develop with consistency concerning the brand's culture and identity. The most critical and challenging challenge is instilling ethical values, environmental sustainability, and social responsibility already in the brand's brand identity.

Therefore, define brand equity and an identity strategy in which the ethical approach is an integral and structural part of the brand identity and not a mere impromptu action, for example, the casual participation in some charity initiative, which would risk being interpreted by consumers as not credible, because it is inconsistent with the founding identity of the brand.

## 21.3 Brand Marketing Trends

Let's check out how people's behavior changes and how these complex processes taking place in society affect brands' existence.

Over the past few years, spent on the hype wave, people have started to get tired of the Internet. Psychologists note a tendency manifested in a person's desire to slow down his life. Less and less essential is attached to the noise around; people return to realizing the importance of living their own lives.

## People's Behavior Changes

Fear, instilled in us by the era of the heyday of social networks, FOMO (fear of missing out) is the fear of missing events from the lives of friends or strangers, which pushes us to check the news feeds, becomes a habit and forces us to be aware of all events, recedes. It is replaced by JOMO (joy of missing out), the joy of missing events that do not concern you personally.

Being out of trend is no longer so scary. Slow traffic culture is gaining more and more popularity. Within its framework, there are already many subcultures: slow city, slow aging, slow food, slow fashion, etc.

Before our eyes, a cultural revolution is taking place, the motto of which is the statement "faster is not always better." The point is not to unnaturally slow down the course of life, but to live at the right speed.

Most brands are still far from understanding and accepting these changes in society. They, like the most extensive social platforms, still perceive users as an application to the interface. Today, many people have realized all the personal lapses from the waste of time on social networks. They want new experiences, even from their gadgets.

Of course, at this level, people are not ready to completely abandon social networks. Still, they want to use these resources for what they were intended for, communicating within their community.

For brands, this means it's time to stop thinking of social media as a place to target ads correctly. It's time to develop real interaction: less content, more contact.

## Music as Part Of The Brand Image

Music is a unique language. She can tell an incredible amount. With its help, we define our own and others.

Music is the key today. And the tech brands were the first to realize this. Brands from all categories are now joining them. Recently, we've seen more companies integrate this international language into their image. If you're looking to engage a younger audience, the right music can be the determining factor.

## User-Generated Content as A Creative Component of the Brand

Many brands that have been developing content marketing for several years have not figured out if their investment has paid off. They create a significant amount of overloaded corporate content, precisely the one that most users skip.

Influential brands follow a different strategy; they focus on their targeted audience's interests and rarely talk about themselves. They also attract opinion leaders and, most importantly, clients themselves to cooperate.

Instead of developing content that no one reads, and the return on which is almost impossible to measure, try to evoke emotions from potential customers and motivate them to create their brand content.

Discussion about new technologies

What are the topics actively discussed in business communities?

- Artificial intelligence,
- Voice search,
- Augmented reality,
- Cryptocurrencies,
- Automation.

We love to discuss these topics with colleagues. But why not discuss them with clients? Don't panic; talk about how new technology can improve their lives and invite people to participate in the discussion.

**Avoiding Annoying Ads**

It looks like advertising will soon become an art. An increasing number of brands realize how important a creative and non-trivial approach to their promotion is. We clear the space around us, kitsch and bad taste are a thing of the past.

And if it's quite challenging to fight for a complete victory over aggressive offline and TV advertising formats, everything still depends on the taste of the brand representatives; then, new times are coming online.

# CONCLUSION

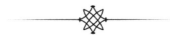

At the end of this journey, we have seen what a brand is. We have analyzed the constitutive elements of a brand's identity. We talked about the positioning of a brand and the aspects that contribute to creating a brand's value.

It is worthy to note that a brand is nothing more than your customer's feelings and memories with your brand. It's an emotional connection between him and your company.

In this definition, it becomes clear that you should approach the matter with a lot of sensitivity. That doesn't necessarily mean that it has to be gentle. Your brand and your customer must be emotionally on the same wavelength. This means that every contact with your company is an experience that is useful for it, be it a good feeling or concrete help. Then your customer is also happy to hear from you and does not feel disturbed.

How do you do that by appearing so that your desired customer is enthusiastic and can identify with it? Be the biggest for your target group, and you will stand out from the crowd. Do it all right, and you are insignificant to everyone.

Is it worth building a brand as a sole proprietorship?

Yes. A company is just an abstract entity. That's why you have to give it a face so that customers (and employees) can develop a relationship with the brand and identify with the company: a corporate personality. This brand identity is a consciously created personality that should harmonize as well as possible with the target group.

As an entrepreneur, you already bring your personality with you. Your entrepreneurial personality is, of course, different from you as a private person. The two characters are closely interwoven, but your entrepreneurial personality also has a consciously created identity. So the differences to the corporate brand are not that great.

Even if you act as a sole trader under your name, you benefit from consciously shaping your image. A brand fulfills many functions. The five most important are:

### Recognition

When you hold a Cola bottle in your hands, you can tell immediately whether it is Coca-Cola or Pepsi. You don't even have to see the logo to do this. With the shape of the bottle, the red color, the white curve, it is immediately apparent which brand is behind it. An outstanding corporate design makes it possible.

### Professionalism

Before your customers can recognize your brand, they will admire the professionalism of your appearance. People judge a book by its cover. And if that looks bumbling, they expect the content to be the same.

### Quality Promise

What the farmer does not know, he does not eat. Behind a brand, there is always a promise of quality that, in case of doubt, is the decisive factor in the purchase decision. Eye-tracking studies have even shown that customers can identify the brands they know from a range of goods at a glance and then choose them preferentially.

### Price Advantage

Yes, establishing a brand costs money. The investment is worthwhile; however, creating a brand can provide significant price advantages. A professional appearance alone makes it easier to enforce higher prices. You can achieve even higher margins if there is a promise of quality behind it that other brands cannot offer.

**ID**

That is the supreme discipline of branding: When the customer knows the brand and recognizes what it stands for. Or even want to adorn themselves with the values of the brand.

Finally, organizations must know how to manage crises carefully; the answers' tones are fundamental; if an organization attacks a single consumer, all out of solidarity, they will defend the weaker subject. To not damage their reputation, the dialogue is critical; indeed, not the only necessary condition, in fact, for one good reputation are essential products to the height and behavior that support the goodness of such products.

We'd be glad to hear from you as you Craft and Design an Irresistible Story Brand Business from this guide.

Cheers:)